Veronica,
Truly apprec



# BABA AND THE CREW

positive energy & insight
on the Kemet journey

## A True Story of a Single Black Father's Journey to Redemption

Keep Building your
Legacy

**Bill Davis, Jr.**

**Foreword by Sekou Babatunde Davis**

Peace & Blessings

Bill

8/24

Printed in the United States of America
2020 First Edition
10 9 8 7 6 5 4 3 2 1

Subject Index:
Davis, William, Jr.
Title: BABA and The Crew: A True Story of Single Black Father's Journey to Redemption
1. Black Fatherhood 2. Family 3. Africana Studies 4. Parenting 5. Civil Rights Movement 6. Paul Robeson 7. Rutgers University

Paperback ISBN: 978-0-578-70163-9
Library of Congress Card Catalog Number: 2020910449

www.babaslegacy.com

BABA'S LEGACY LLC

# PRAISES FOR BABA...

"What makes *Baba and the Crew* special is that it dispels the myth of the absent Black father. It goes against the erroneous stereotypical notion that single-parent families, headed by Black fathers, can hold a family together. It shows the Black father has love, cares for, and has hopes and dreams for his family as much as any other culture.

*Baba and the Crew* demonstrates that a Black father raising a family guided by an Afrocentric framework of loving and caring for his children has the same positive and successful outcome as any group. Bill's story proves that love, hard work, and faith can overcome any obstacles.

I have known Bill Davis and his family for many years and often wondered what his secret was to raising such a good family as a single parent. On many occasions, I have asked him to tell me his secret. He has often said to me, "there is no secret," yet I always felt he was holding something back. After reading *Baba and the Crew*, I realized that he answered my question whenever I asked. This story shows love, caring, and providing for Black children can have the same positive outcome for all children."

**Bruce S. Morgan**

**1st VP New Jersey State Conference NAACP**

**President New Brunswick Area Branch NAACP**

"In our cultural climate of African American inequality, mass incarceration, and racism, *Baba and The Crew* is a great example to eradicate the myth of absentee or deadbeat African American fathers. Bill Davis has taken on his role as Baba, the Swahili term for father, with love, courage, and determination to raise and equip his children with the knowledge, compassion, and tools to thrive in society. He shows readers that gender stereotypes of men not being emotionally available or capable of taking care of children is false. Bill's story is one that needs to be highlighted more often in mass media."

**Dr. Randal Pinkett**

**Chairman and CEO, BCT Partners and**

**Co-author, *Black Faces in White Places***

"The story of *Baba and the Crew* is one of determination, love of family, inspiration, and endurance. It is the story of a father who used his own experiences as a child of the sixties, his knowledge of teenage pregnancies that permeated generations of his family members, to form his parenting style. Baba was overly protective of his Crew out of a desire to break the cycle of teenage pregnancies. This is the story of a father's unconditional love for his children, a father who knew the value of education, and the need for his Crew to be well-grounded in the culture and wisdom of the ancestors. Baba used structure, discipline, and love to build a tribe of strong, independent, and educated men and women capable of standing on their own in a world that is not always kind to melanated people. His familial bonding lessons are like guiding posts for his Crew to get to a place of solace and support when necessitated by life's journeys. As a father raising his Crew, by himself, Baba shows the reader what is possible when embracing a commitment to fatherhood in all its forms and dimensions. This story of a Black father's journey on his road to redemption is a lesson for all Black men; it shows that love can conquer all and that Black men can be great fathers, against the odds."

**Honorable Adrian O. Mapp**
**Mayor, Plainfield New Jersey**

"In a time when American society yet devalues Afrocentric manhood, and American media yet denigrates Afrocentric fatherhood, Bill Davis and his four highly accomplished children debunk both maladies. The 'must-read,' **Baba and the Crew: A True Story of a Single Black Father's Journey to Redemption**, chronicles the remedy to overcome one of slavery's lingering egregious legacies for single-parent African American families--the decision, by God's grace, to make it anyhow! Indeed, Bill Davis' praxis journey reveals that vigilant, principle-based child-rearing, coupled with a healthy portion of wisdom and empathy, more often than not, has been the accurate historical narrative for Afrocentric fathers in America. Thus, I highly recommend this book to ALL fathers, regardless of ethnicity or marital status, who cherish their children and hope to bequeath to our nation a potent legacy through them, as Bill Davis has!"

**Rev. Dr. W. Golden Carmon, Sr.**
Senior Pastor, Mt. Zion A.M.E. Church
New Brunswick, NJ 08901

"In this revealing memoir, "Baba" Bill shares not only his parenthood journey, but he also demonstrates the extent to which childhood experiences, and the way we are parented, shape the way we decide to parent. Without rancor, recrimination, or braggadocio, Bill assesses, with great objectivity—and clarity, the generational parenting behaviors in his family he chose to emulate while rearing his own children and those he diligently strove to avoid. Bill did not elect single fatherhood, but when life dealt him those cards, he took up the "Baba" challenge with a loving, willing determination to do everything in his power to make sure he had a winning hand. While this memoir looks back at family history and moves forward toward the family's future, it is grounded solidly in the present lives of Baba and his Crew. This is not a parenting primer or "how-to" guide from an "expert" but rather an unflinchingly honest, self-effacing, and sometimes humorous, behind-the-scenes look at how this single father raised four children to be culturally centered, kind, aspirational, compassionate, critical thinking, self-reliant adults."

**Virginia DeBerry, NY Times Best-selling Author**

"I strongly endorse Prof. Bill Davis' book. He was my former undergraduate student at Rutgers College, and I had the great pleasure of calling him Bill "Black" Davis. He was a very good student and became an outstanding father and single parent to high achieving children. I remember seeing him, with his children, on the television show—Reading Rainbow, as he represented a strong role model as a Black father and single parent. He managed to have a successful career, balancing home duties, and challenging work. His children turned out to be outstanding adults and strong role models for the African American community. As a former Chair and faculty member of the Rutgers Department of Africana Studies (i.e., serving 45 years before retiring and being granted "Professor Emeritus"), it gave me great pleasure to have Prof. Bill Davis as a colleague teaching in Africana Studies. This book will be a significant contribution to the Black community, Rutgers University, and positive Black male image."

**Dr. Leonard L. Bethel**
**Professor Emeritus**
**Rutgers University, NJ**

"*Baba and the Crew: A True Story of a Single Black Father's Journey Redemption,* by Bill Davis, Jr., is well-worth reading during this time when all attention is on the murder of George Floyd and the resurgence of the Black Lives Matter movement.

Bill Davis' commitment as a single father stemmed from the lessons learned from his parents, especially his mother. Bill raised his children in a strict rules-enforced environment, yet he gave them a sense of pride in their cultural heritage and encouraged them to read and seek and speak the truth. He also instilled within his children the belief education was a key element to their success. His children knew from birth that their names had significant meanings. Whenever anyone asked his children their names, they articulated their names and their names' meanings. Bill describes their initial reluctance in this public display, and how later it became transformative for the children to listen to each other during this practice.

Being a single father when the mother is not deceased is not necessarily a common phenomenon. Bill sculpts a plan for other Black men to follow in raising their children, especially if single parenting.

One of the quotes Bill Davis uses by W.E.B. DuBois summarizes the essence of Bill Davis' book, "Children learn more from what you are than what you teach." As a single parent, Bill's lifestyle was to demonstrate through his actions and words his love for his "Crew." He

lived the family values he wanted them to learn by attending all their activities, working hard, and being a proud Black father and man. He loved his "crew" with agape love. Bill Davis' children learned to love their father and one another and their neighbor because of their father's love for them. "I wanted to read more."
**Rev. Dr. Deborah L. Stapleton**

"Bill Davis' memoir is a tribute to the reality and normalcy of strong Black men with authentic family values. Here is a testament to Black Fatherhood that prevails against all racist and financial odds. It should be read by young Black men and women as a necessary Rite of Passage into Black Adulthood—especially in these protracted trying times.

Bill Davis created a way out of no way for a model family to use as a template to redefine and re-establish strong Black Families that are neither matriarchal nor patriarchal, but beautifully loving families that are flexible enough to bend with the ill winds and still proudly grow."
**s. e. anderson**
***author of The Black Holocaust for Beginners***

"The much-used saying "It takes a village to raise a child" has a new meaning, thanks to Bill Davis Jr. In his new book, *Baba and the Crew*, he shares his incredible journey as a single Black father who refused to give up on his children. It's a heartwarming blueprint on fatherhood with practical advice & reminders of the power of love, forgiveness, and transformation.

*Baba and the Crew* is a blueprint for single fathers raising their children in the wake of uncertainty & amid today's common parental

challenges. Thank you, Bill Davis Jr., for sharing your journey of redemption, fatherhood lessons, and the sacred values you used to guide your children. In a society where negative stereotypes of Black fathers are the norm, Bill Davis Jr. provides readers with a much-needed archetype. He emerges as a positive role model for all fathers."
**Caryl Lucas, Author, Speaker & Life Coach**

"When I first met Bill Davis in 1997, I was the Superintendent of the Piscataway school system. Bill was a single Dad who was extremely active in the community. Bill's main concern that I shared was the underperforming African-American students in the Piscataway school system. We worked together to achieve the beginning of turning that around in Piscataway. Bill was also extremely helpful in the recruitment of minority candidates in the Piscataway school system. With his help, we made strides in achievement, but we also brought more diversity to the professional staff of Piscataway. We were the first school district to employ a student advocate in the high school whose primary job was to advocate for students who did not have a voice. I went to the Plainfield school system in 2019. I was fortunate to work with Bill, who continued to advocate for African American and Latino students who had been neglected academically. Over the years, I got to know Bill, not only for his success with students but as a proud father of five highly successful graduates of Rutgers University. What always impressed me about Bill was his ability to advocate for others, and maintain his love and guidance for his five children. That balance is a role model for all single fathers. I am honored to have Bill in my life as someone I can rely on to be supportive, provide guidance, and honestly tell me what more I could do for students. Of all Bill's accomplishments, I most admire him as a devoted father."

**Ronald E. Bolandi Former Piscataway Twp.**
**Superintendent of Schools**

"Bill Davis's story stands in stark contrast to the dominant narrative around black fathers. This book is an inspiration for all parents, and the advice that Brother Bill provides will help you raise your children to become strong adults. While being honest about the challenges facing black families, each chapter is also uplifting and filled with the positive energy we all need to prepare our young people to thrive in this world."

**LeDerick Horne**
**Poet, Disability Activist**

# DEDICATION

To my parents, Charlotte and Bill. I appreciate all of your love and lessons that have made me the man and parent I have become. I also dedicate this book to my Crew, Sekou, Toussaint, Imani, and Naeemah—I will always love you; you have and continue to be the wind beneath my wings—keep rising.

Also, to all fathers, especially African American men, who, despite the many challenges, continue to do your best by loving and supporting your children.

AFRICA

# AUTHORS NOTE

The names of a few key people in my life have been changed to protect their privacy.

AFRICA

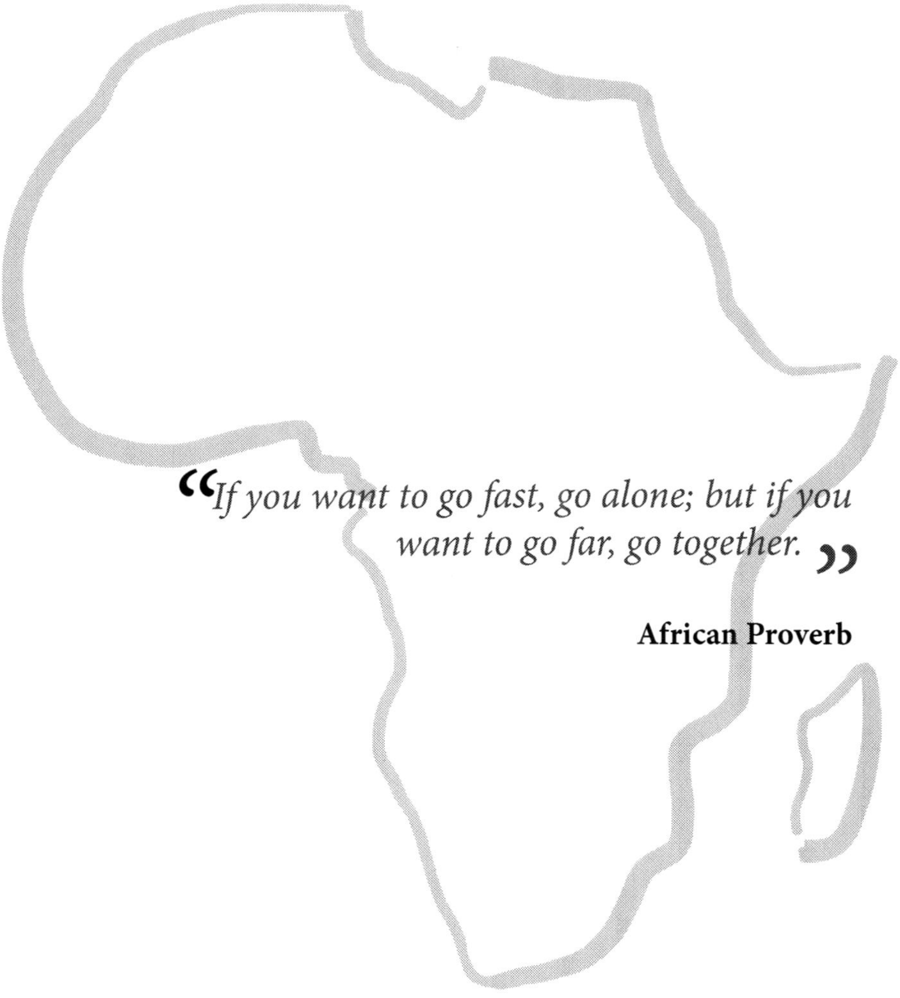

*"If you want to go fast, go alone; but if you want to go far, go together."*

**African Proverb**

AFRICA

# TABLE OF CONTENTS

Dedication ..... xi

Authors Note ..... xii

Acknowledgments ..... xvii

Foreword ..... xviii

Prologue ..... xxiii

It's A Family Affair ..... xxvi

Introduction ..... xxviii

**Part I: Sonship ..... 1**

Chapter 1: Brick City Debut ..... 4

Chapter 2: Actin' Up ..... 8

Chapter 3: Black Rebellion ..... 13

Chapter 4: Motivation ..... 17

Chapter 5: Brother Black ..... 24

**Part II: Fatherhood ..... 29**

Chapter 6: Something In Common ..... 30

Chapter 7: Sekou ..... 33

Chapter 8: Toussaint ..... 47

AFRICA

Chapter 9: Imani .... 60

Chapter 10: Naeemah .... 70

Chapter 11: Flying Solo .... 83

Chapter 12: Trouble Ahead .... 89

Chapter 13: Ripples In The Pond .... 98

**Familia .... 109**

**Part III: Redemption .... 141**

Chapter 14: Baba Crew Evaluations .... 142

Chapter 15: Thicker Than Water .... 185

Chapter 16: My Redemption Song .... 197

Epilogue .... 200

About The Author .... 202

Further Acknowledgments .... 205

Resources .... 206

Endnotes .... 211

# ACKNOWLEDGMENTS

In writing this book, I would like to acknowledge my sisters Jean and Barbara, my brother Marshall, and my late brother Kevin—we are the 5 Tots; let us, aka lettuce continue to honor Mom and Daddy. A very special thank you to Aunt Willa. I really appreciate you and your support.

I would like to thank Everett Lattimore, my first track coach, posthumously. His example and encouragement kept me on "the right track." And a very special thank you to Ron Upperman, who encouraged me and many members of the team and me to aim to be our best. To all of the members of our "village;" and we have a "hell of a village;" there are too many to name, but some need to be highlighted: Willie and Val, I love y'all and genuinely appreciate your friendship and support. Albert and Evette, your love and support have been a blessing. LeDerick my brother, continue to rise; your talent and example are needed more than ever. Bruce and Debbie, "the Prez and 1st lady," your love and support and leadership example have been very beneficial to the community. Paul and Karen, thanks for being great neighbors and Paul, a special thanks for DJ-ing my ol' fashion house parties. Alex Gray, Mo Lucky, Pam Travis, Lydia Troutman, Crossroads, Educational Opportunity Fund (EOF), and ASTEP and PROJECT ACCESS Staff, teachers, counselors, coaches, and mentors, I sincerely appreciate your efforts and contributions to guiding 'the Crew' through the school and community activities.

# FOREWORD

## "I'M AWAKE…
## I'M ALIVE…
## AND I FEEL GREAT!"

Those eight words were our daily affirmation growing up. Each morning, Baba would join us in this chant around the house, providing everyone with the motivation and energy needed to begin our daily routine. At the time, I didn't quite understand how powerful this action was for all of us, most importantly, Baba. How else would a single father of four gather the strength needed to raise us every day? Becoming a father has helped me fully appreciate how these eight simple words shaped my parenting style.

No one woke up earlier than Baba. Our house filled with classic R&B as well as occasional handclaps and whistles. Baba set the tone each day, maintaining a familiar rhythm that we all became accustomed to. This routine was important for all of us to operate on schedule – there was not much room for improvisation. Baba's disciplined and structured nature are traits that I now value, as difficult as these lessons were growing up. I absolutely see the benefit of establishing routines with my six-year-old daughter, Nia. I have the privilege of waking her up each day in a similar fashion. Although the soundtrack has been slightly updated, our daily routine shares the same essence as my upbringing.

No one sacrificed more than Baba. The Crew always came first. When decisions were made, if they were not going to benefit our whole family, they did not happen. During our summer vacations, I'm sure Baba would have preferred to fly instead of drive. But economically, the Davis road trip just made much more sense at the time. I'm also sure that we worked his last nerve on these excursions! How Baba financially managed to handle the essentials AND afford a trip to Disney? To this day, I have no idea! What I've come to understand is that forgoing certain personal comforts to see your children live their dreams is priceless. Nia once told her friend, "you know, we live a pretty awesome life." I'll never forget the conviction she had behind that statement, how happy and alive she looked at that moment. I smiled and thought to myself how grateful I am that Baba taught me through his actions how to become more selfless.

I heard Baba once say that being a father is the most challenging and rewarding job he'll ever have. Now that the Crew is all grown up, I am confident he can look back on this journey with a sense of pride. In fact, I know that Baba feels redeemed by how things turned out. He spoke this into existence over 25 years ago! So, Baba, thank you. Thank you for your profound impact on my life, my siblings' lives, and the countless village members you've touched directly with your words or indirectly with your spirit.

In December 2010, I was flat broke. I had to humbly move back into Baba's house, and the pressure to earn a living was immense. Not to mention, Kwanzaa and Baba's birthday were on the horizon. I couldn't afford to buy Baba a gift, but I had the idea to record my own tribute song. The concept was to interpolate Tupac's "Dear Mama" and create a celebration of Baba's life. To give him the flowers while he can still smell them, I created "Dear Baba:"

*I take this time out to reminisce*
*Though all the drama, I can always depend on Baba*
*He came in the world back in '54*
*Who would've thought that this Wednesday would've meant so much more?*
*As the firstborn son, he would be the one to carry on the name junior*
*William Henry the Ruler*
*As a preschooler, he was always the cooler, smoother*
*Ahead of his time like computers*
*Then he started elementary, hey*
*Knowing that would be his destiny one day*
*Kept his nose in the books man that's right*
*Mom taught him to appreciate his black side*
*And even as a young teen, Baba*
*You always had big dreams, Baba*
*Coming from a man I just hope you understand*
*You are appreciated*

***Hook:***
*Billy, don't you know we love you*
*Billy, place no one above you*

*He moved up outta Blue Bell*
*Knew damn well had to blaze him a new trail*
*Plainfield took him to new heights*

*Shining star underneath all the bright lights*
*Basketball and track, yea he excelled at*
*Almost ran out to Cali but then he fell back*
*The revolution wouldn't be televised*
*P-funk took on a new vibe*
*Brother Black now was his new name*
*Legend of Malcolm X running through his veins*
*'72 would start a new era*
*Founded SAS and made the scene better*
*Stand up, say yes, we are proud now*
*No more time to waste no more lying down*
*The black voice got a little base to it*
*Student leadership got a new face to it*
*You see, you are the inspiration*
*That's why I had to write this dedication*
*And there's no way they can pay you back*
*But the plan is to show you that I understand*
*You are appreciated*

**Hook:**
*Billy, don't you know we love you*
*Billy, place no one above you*

*And all my childhood memories*
*Are full of all the sweet things you did for me*
*Remember taking road trips cross country*
*Are we there yet, Baba I'm real hungry?*
*Not for knowledge, c'mon man we talking food*

*Boy eat that grapefruit it's good for you*
*Ah man, here we go again*
*When I didn't listen, and a whipping was the only way to make me understand*
*But then, when I dropped out*
*And the school of life was the only class I cared about*
*You still supported even though it seemed crazy*
*Thinking this music would pay me*
*And I can't wait till I see the day*
*When we can send you on your private island getaway*
*You always were committed*
*A black, single father with four kids tell me how you did it*
*For your 57$^{th}$ birthday*
*Davis family made the world say*
*There's no way I can pay you back*
*But my plan is to show you that I understand*

*Baba, I love you.*

# PROLOGUE

*Keep the faith (Imani):*
*Give thanks and praises to the Creator and ancestors for the blessings and challenges of being a parent. Despite the challenges, I will be able to honor the legacy of Black parents who came before me and who have overcome much worse, including mom and daddy. The Creator has blessed me and the "Crew" with excellent health, food on the table, and a clean, safe place to live. I love my Crew. Although at times, growing up, it may not have seemed like it to them.*

*Sekou, my oldest son, had many talents at his young age: intelligence, artistic, and athletic—a triple threat. Keeping him on task has been a considerable challenge. Toussaint, my second son, is very kind and caring. With his warm personality, he quickly made friends, yet he was shy and embarrassed by his stuttering. He has become the "tallest tree" in our forest. Imani, the first girl, was always very insightful for her age—she is her mother's child. Shifting to being raised by me without her mother has impacted all of them, but she expresses it the most. Naeemah, the baby girl, is trying to find her way being the last of the Crew. She has already overcome a severe health crisis, which gives me hope that she has the fighting spirit and will make an excellent path for herself.*

*Upon reflection, seeing their smiles and listening to them sing and play when they were younger made me happy and determined to keep them safe. There have been some painful family lessons that we're not going to repeat. The main one is to end the pattern of multi-generational teenage parenting. This reality has had a profound impact on our family, among others. My mother and grandmother and my sisters and brothers, including me, became teenage parents. My mother dropped out of high school to take care of my sister. She eventually completed her GED, but clearly, she could have accomplished more; this was a valuable lesson I learned late. Being a teenage parent also limits or makes it very difficult to achieve educational and professional dreams. I've had many conversations with the Crew about this, and thankfully they have listened.*

*I prayed to the Creator and ancestors to guide me and the Crew since I never had a back-up plan. My prayer was always to stay healthy, so they would not end up in foster care or split up with the boys and or girls raised by other family members. I've tried to live my dreams, not my fears. It hasn't been easy. I've read different inspirational books, listened to music, and talk shows to keep my spirits up; sometimes it works, other times it doesn't. Listening to the Sounds of Blackness, "Optimistic," helped me keep the faith and gave me the strength to keep going. Knowing the difficulties on the horizon, including racism and sexism, they are going to face was a great challenge. Figuring out how to prepare them for life's realities and not break their spirit was also difficult.*

*When I decided to write about my life, Bob Marley's "Redemption Song," always came to mind. Especially the lyrics, "emancipate yourself from mental slavery – none but ourselves can free our mind." This lyric is one of the fundamental principles that I think I wanted to instill in my children and one that we should all embrace. We've been fed false narratives about who we are as Black people for far too long. Honoring the legacy of our ancestors will be a significant accomplishment and essential to navigating through life.*

*Making breakfast, washing clothes, going to work, and taking the 'Crew' to school and their activities were more than I anticipated. I needed help early on, but I wasn't sure how to get it. I had to learn to put my ego in my pocket and ask for help. I was thankful that I was able to "build a village"– especially for Imani and Naeemah who needed to see and spend time with positive women. There have been a few folks who were willing to help—thank goodness. Their compassion took the sting off of numerous rejections. Many people are surprised when we show up without their mother. The curious looks and the questions in their eyes asking, 'what happened?' Sometimes I wonder myself.*

*The needs of children increase as they age, and the need to be engaged as a parent becomes more critical. As children desire to be more independent, parents must find the balance to support their growth, and ensure the choices they make are healthy, reinforcing the need for a 'village.' Having other adults who can strengthen the parents' message is significant. All of us are better when people encourage us to honor our best selves. Just as we had to face peer pressure, our children face this challenge; and there are both negative and positive influences. Unfortunately, the negative seems to be more fun for children, even if it presents a danger. There are many lessons I have taught them, and I have done so, in my opinion, with patience, and other times I have not been as patient if the lesson is one that could lead to detrimental results. I am fortunate that my children have realized that those early life lessons were worth their weight in gold. Despite their initial sadness about me raising all of them without their mother, they now have a better understanding of the situation and realize that it was the redemptive choice.*

*Yea yea yea, the Creator, has a master plan to bring peace and justice through all the land. Peace and happiness through all the land.*

*Keep the faith and stay strong,*

*Bill "Brother Black" Davis 2/20/20*

# It's a Family Affair

My child grows up to be
Happy and healthy
All of the children grow up to be
Role models in the community

Sekou gave us rhythm and rhyme
A beat to keep us in time

Toussaint the tallest tree
Helped us to see greater possibility

Imani gave us faith and leadership
Guided us all along

Naeemah helped us to Dream
Inspired us to be on the scene

Grand Mom and Big Bunk
Gave us love and encouragement

Yes we are family
I got all my children with me

AFRICA

They are the wind beneath my wings
My heroes and sheroes

We have gone far because we have gone together
We will always be together forever

# INTRODUCTION

*"I was determined to find a way to take care of my children even though everyone in my circle thought I was crazy."*

\- ***Bill Davis***

I am a proud Baba. Each of my children has called me Baba since birth. "Baba" means father in several African languages, and the name is associated with a high level of respect for your role and responsibility as the man of the house. I wanted my children to have a strong cultural foundation on their journey in life from the beginning. I was intentional and did not want them to prescribe to all of the distractions and negative stereotypes of what society has labeled or deemed what it means to be Black. I wanted my children to be proud of their heritage and the profound work of their ancestors. More importantly, it was essential for me to educate them on Black History with a more in-depth representation and understanding than what is traditionally taught in the school system.

I have raised a tribe, my Crew of four beautiful children: Sekou Keita Babatunde, Toussaint Osiris, Imani Nefertari Simone, and Naeemah Ife Safiya. As children, whenever we were in public, I had them line up by age and say their full name and meaning. Sekou was first in line: "Hi, my name is Sekou Keita Babatunde, and it means one who fights for justice." Toussaint was up next, and he stuttered as a kid, so it took great courage to recite, "Hi, my name is Toussaint Osiris, and I am named after the Haitian leader who fought for the freedom of Haiti." As the third child and the first girl, Imani was out to prove that she could do anything better than her brothers. "Hi, my name is Imani Nefertari Simone. I'm named after the seventh principle of Kwanzaa, which means faith to family and community, and it is the name of an Egyptian Queen. Coming up the rear was Naeemah, who would quickly say her name to get it over with, "Hi, I'm Naeemah Ife Safiya, and my name means benevolence (grace), loved wise one.

Back then, they all regarded the Davis kid's formation as pure torture. Today, they are all incredibly proud of their names, and so am I. If it were not for the respect and admiration I have for my father, William Davis, Sr., I would have adopted the name Sekou myself. In hindsight, I realize that I was putting my children on a public stage, which caused Toussaint and Naeemah anxiety. I used this type of exercise to encourage their communication, eye contact, and social skills at a young age. In the long run, I think it helped all of them become more comfortable speaking to others.

I wanted to be present at all of my children's athletic and academic milestones. When I was growing up and ran track in junior high and high school, my mom only came to *one* track meet. That experience instilled my commitment to be a hands-on father at all of my children's extracurricular activities. In our house, academics were first and foremost, yet all four involved sports, band, arts, and community. I ensured that they prescribed to the Paul Robeson legacy—academics, athletics, arts, and social justice. At times, we were like our own home team package: my sons played pop warner football, my daughters were cheerleaders, and I was the play-by-play announcer. We were a true family unit. We ate dinner together *every* night, with very few exceptions. Consistency and stability were essential to me. My primary goal was to create a stable environment of love, discipline, respect, and above all, family first.

I also wanted my children to value black history, so I provided an environment to embrace who they are. I am convinced that the value of black history had a significant impact when they were younger. I felt it was imperative to create family traditions of love and togetherness to strengthen the bonds when they got older. Kwanzaa became a vital family tradition because I was skeptical about the commercialization of Christmas, and a white Santa Claus never resonated with me. I had to find ways to help my children understand who they are and what we are collectively trying to accomplish in this journey.

My Crew and I have come a long way. If it were not for the village, our family first mantra, and our commitment to the process, we might have had more challenges. I was determined to find a way to take care of my children. No one in my circle thought it was a good idea to take my children on this single father path without their mother. Most people thought I was crazy—some actually said it to my face and shook their heads as if they wanted nothing to do with me after my decision. I can only imagine the negative things that others said behind my back.

Yes, I made a lot of mistakes along the way. Early on, I was ashamed to ask for help, but I found the courage to put my ego in check and connected with strong women and families willing to help as necessary. Although my parenting style was strict, it was done with the utmost love and the best intentions to give my children a chance at a successful future. Now that they are adults, our family connection remains strong. Even though everyone is living their lives in New Jersey, New York, and Oregon, we stay in close contact with each other via family chat videos, emails, and group texts. My Crew even has their sibling chat to talk about things they don't want Baba to know. Fortunately, we are all better human beings because of our love for one another and our desire to see each other succeed. I consider myself blessed to be able to sit back and watch my Crew mature and navigate life based on their upbringing.

I'm not sure when or where I learned that being consistent was a much-needed skill as a parent, but fortunately, it's a lesson I've lived by for many years. When people ask me what works, I reply, "being consistent with our expectations and reinforcement are high on my list." What also helps is having a vision for their future, that is larger than children can ever imagine for themselves. Both can be daunting, but they are necessary. More importantly, in our household, we maintained the balance of practicing Maat, the philosophy of our ancient Egyptian ancestors. Maat represents exhibiting each person's ethical and moral principles daily by acting with honor and truth in the areas of family, community, and the environment.

This book is truly my redemption song. My redemption is being a single Black father overcoming obstacles and barriers while witnessing my children bear fruit due to my sacrifices. Despite the sociological research documenting Black fathers' significant level of engagement with their children, stereotypes of Black men as lazy deadbeat dads, thugs, and womanizers, still shape popular perceptions. My purpose in writing *Baba and The Crew* is to present a positive image of fatherhood despite my adversity and shortcomings. I hope to demystify the cloud over single Black fatherhood as if it is this "weird" anomaly and demonstrate that it is a possible and necessary role in the Black community and society at large. Far too many grandmothers have taken on duties as grandma and daddy to our children.

Parenting presents daily challenges, even when your children become adults. It's definitely a fine line between when to push and when to give them space, when to adjust, and how to encourage your child to fail forward. Most of all, to emphasize that you love them even when they can't accomplish a particular goal. Since the Creator has blessed us with good health, knowledge, and opportunities for growth, the Davis Crew will be fine. And yes, I will always be a proud Baba.

# PART I
# Sonship

*"My father's view of fatherhood shaped my view of how fatherhood should be."*
**- Bill Davis**

**Dedicated to my mother, Charlotte Davis**

***Ode to Charlotte With Love***

Never would have made it, never would have made it without you
Mom, we never would have made it without you
Your care & natural hair
Your courage & common sense
sometimes very intense
Helped us keep our sense

Our sense of pride helped to guide us through
The challenges you knew all of us had to go through
Questions about sanity & humanity

With your wisdom & insight, you made sure our world was right
Daddy was right
You are the 'general'
Following in the Harriet tradition
Leading us to a better position

With your grace and style, you loved us all the while
Listening to Sam Cooke and Nina Simone
Teaching us to be young gifted & black
Cause you knew that's where it's at
You & Dad have joined them as ancestors
But this poem is a tribute to you
We just wanted you to know we love you so
And we never would have made it without you
*Rip, 2009*

**Dedicated to my father, William Davis, Sr.**

***All Hail to the Emperor***

If there was ever a man who was generous gracious and good, that was my dad the Man
A human being so true he could live his life as a king cause he knew the real treasure in life
The Man, Big Bunk, The Emperor
The Man with a plan always willing to share and care and
To Dare
To be free from the stereotypes of this society
He was a Black man who took care of his clan - children - grand and great grand
He left us the other day
He had other worlds to go see
You must understand he was the Emperor of the Universe
He's traveling with Duke on the 'A' train to transverse and converse
About a love supreme
To live like he should live to live like a King
And be free again
We love you Emperor
*RIP 3/28/03*

# CHAPTER 1

# BRICK CITY DEBUT

*"I am what time, circumstance, history, have made of me, certainly, but I am also so much more than that. So are we all."*

**— James Baldwin**

I was born in Presbyterian Hospital in Newark, New Jersey Central Ward District to Charlotte Hall and William Henry Davis. As the first son, I was named after my father, William Henry Davis. Daddy had high expectations for all of us, especially me, as his namesake. He served in the Navy as a cook during World War II and was always very open about racism and discrimination that Blacks faced fighting for a country that didn't value us as human beings. The military adhered to Jim Crow segregation, and Black men served in support roles as a cook, quartermaster, and gravediggers.

My grandfather died when my father was around seven years old, so my dad never had a male role model during his childhood. However, he told me stories of how he always imagined being a great father someday. On a scale of 1-10, I give him a nine because he "whopped" my a_ _ hundreds of times. I guess I deserved it because he repeatedly said, "Why are you so damned hard-headed?"

Daddy was 5'7" and 160 pounds with a similar Billy Dee Williams mustache and swag. His skin was a glowing caramel brown without a blemish, and a dimple on his right cheek. He was proud of his thick black wavy hair that could be easily combed back into the "conk" hairstyle without having to get a lye relaxer like his buddies that burned their scalp like hell. Daddy was popular, and the neighborhood folks referred to him as "Pretty Bill." More importantly, he was the quintessential romantic. He loved romantic music and always wanted to visit Venice because it was a place for "lovers."

I admired my dad because he read two or three newspapers each day: *The Star-Ledger*, *The Newark Evening News*, and *The New York Times*. Daddy was conversant about a myriad of national topics and kept abreast of world affairs. He was present in all of our lives and taught us about history, current events, how to cook, fix cars, cut grass, paint, and gamble, to name a few. Gambling was an integral part of his life. He won big and lost big, yet never lost the itch.

I don't recall how my parents met, but my mom had my sister Jean before they got together. Then my sister Barbara came a year after Jean. During the marriage, I was the firstborn son, and then 14 months later, my brother Kevin came along. Kevin had asthma and was fragile growing up, so he got all of the lap time and pity points. My parents' relationship was complicated. They both had extramarital affairs, yet they respected each other and did their best to raise us as a nuclear family. There was never any question of half-brother or half-sister. A few years later, my mom had my younger brother, Marshall, from another man. Again, Daddy regarded all five of us as *his* children. During his time in the military, since he served as a cook, he worked at different restaurants when he got out and learned the restaurant business. He opened a soul food restaurant in Newark called "The Five Tots." None of us kids had chores or involvement in the restaurant, yet it showed daddy's regard for us as a family unit.

Daddy had a great partner in mom, who was also an attractive, self-educated lady. Mom was the seventh child of 14 born in rural Williamstown, New Jersey. Her father died when she was only ten years old. Mom was 5'4" and 140 pounds with a chocolate complexion. Our family hues varied from caramel to chocolate. I was caramel like daddy and mom wanted to make sure that I was clearly not biased toward dark-skinned folks. Mom had been discriminated against by whites and light-skinned Blacks throughout her life and wanted to make sure we were not "color struck." Mom wore her naturally curly, aka kinky hair, with pride. When the Black is Beautiful Movement happened during the 1960s, Mom sported the most beautiful Angela Davis fro. Her Afro-centric influences impacted all of us kids, especially me.

Mom instilled racial pride and frugalness or being responsible with your money. She often fussed with daddy when he took all of us on Sundays to New York for a movie and to eat out. As a chef, he wanted to try signature dishes in reputable restaurants. I don't recall restaurants' names, but as a growing young man, I was happy to eat fancy pasta, seafood, and steaks along the streets of New York City. On the other hand, Mom thought treating all of us to a fancy dinner, and the movie was just a waste of money. She was definitely the matriarch of the house. Daddy called her "the General." She had lots of rules, and if you didn't follow them, it was your behind! As soon as we got home from school, we had to change out of our school clothes. Mom was straight up, no chaser. Her philosophy was, "This is how it is, and there is not much room for debate!" All five of us had daily chores and weekend chores. I had to cut grass, rake leaves, take out the trash, and clean my room. Kevin got off easy because his asthma was something terrible.

Music was an integral part of our home environment, and mom had an unusual taste in music. Nina Simone was among her favorites, as was Ray Charles and Sam Cooke. Whenever I hear "Young, Gifted, and Black," I think of my mom in the kitchen making fried chicken, collard greens, and baked macaroni and cheese. Mom's musical influences still have an impact on my life.

Despite my parents' differences and eventual separation, the most important lesson we learned in the Davis household was to honor and value family. I carried that mantra to my own house and with my Crew.

# CHAPTER 2

# ACTIN' UP

*"Everything will change. The only question is growing up or decaying."*
**— Nikki Giovanni**

My memories of Newark are limited because our family moved to Plainfield in the early 1960s. There are a few potent memories ingrained in my mind, which happened when I was around seven or eight years old. I set a mattress on fire in the junkyard near our house, and one of my friends ratted me out. Fortunately, there was not a lot of damage to any other property. Daddy didn't see it that way. To this day, that whooping from my dad was one to remember. I also got terrible whoopings when I acted up in school, which was usually once or twice a month.

The last memory I have of Newark was on Emmet Street. I was crossing the street without looking and got hit by a car. Thankfully the driver wasn't going fast. I was knocked to the ground. It happened right on my block, so my mother came running to the scene. I remained on the ground until she came. The first thing I said to her was, "Where's my money?"

"Boy, what are you talking about? What money?"

"You know, like Jean. Remember when she got hit by a car, she got thousands! Where's mine?"

"Are you in pain? Where does it hurt? I don't see any bruises."

The owner of the car got out. I could see that she was scared. "Miss, I'm sorry, but your son just came out of nowhere. I did not see him until he was in front of the car. Do you want my information, or are you going to call the police?"

"I'll just take down your information. I think he will be fine."

I was disappointed that I didn't get any money. Not that I would have had access to thousands of dollars anyway. It is great to be young and healthy because I don't recall being sore or having any issues after that incident. I spent the rest of the day misbehaving in the streets with my friends. In hindsight, I realize that all of my acting out during my adolescence was for attention. I was jealous of mom and daddy being at Kevin's beck and call. His terrible wheezing frightened all of us. As we got older, Kevin and I truly bonded. I miss him, dearly. He passed away in 2015.

## Movin' on Up

Our family moved to Plainfield because daddy "hit the number!" I don't know how much money he won, but our lifestyle changed. We moved into a beautiful home on a tree-lined street, and daddy had a baby blue Lincoln Towncar car with navy seats. Daddy became a professional gambler, playing street numbers, betting horses, and playing cards. He believed in betting hard. One of his many great sayings was, "a scared man can't gamble, and a jealous man can't work."

Plainfield was known as the "Queen City" in the 1960s. It was a mixed community economically and racially. Growing up in a multiracial community has both advantages and disadvantages. It helps you learn that you are as talented as everyone else, but you can be discriminated against and not given the needed encouragement or support. It can also help prepare you to face racism. We moved to a mostly white neighborhood, off Berkman Street. It was a significant change from Newark. In our own way, we were among a few other Black families living life like *The Jeffersons*, before George and Weezy came on the scene. Moving the family to a better neighborhood and schools continues to be something that many parents aspire for their children, especially single parents. There are countless stories in the media of single Black moms receiving jail time, probation, and hefty fines for sending their kids to a safer and advanced school district. My parents wanted all of us to have the best opportunity to succeed far beyond their accomplishments.

I got kicked out of school a few times when I was in the fifth or sixth grade. I wanted to do my own thing and was caught walking the halls or just not following class rules. My mom beat me on those occasions and put me on punishment. She actually made me raise my hand in the house to ask permission to go to the bathroom or the kitchen. Mom was determined to instill in me that there were rules that had to be followed, or there would be consequences.

One day I came home for lunch as usual. I did not realize that the principal had called my house to tell my parents about me acting out. Hence, daddy gave me a whoopin' and sent me back to school. I acted up a lot and got more beatings than my brothers and sisters combined. Even though mom and daddy both dropped out of high school, they valued education. My mom proudly completed her GED. There was no question that all of us "five tots" were going to graduate high school. In fact, all of us achieved that goal and made our parents proud. We all attended some college, and I graduated. My late brother Kevin followed daddy's footsteps and graduated from a culinary institute. My sisters Jean and Barbara, started the college route but never finished.

Another early memory in Plainfield was the first time I was called a "nigger." I can still see the look on this white boy named Charles' face when he said it. Charles spoke with a southern drawl and just one day stepped to me and yelled "nigger" and punched me in the face. No one broke us up, and we went to blows. Yes, I "whooped" his a_ _ as we say in the neighborhood, but I ended up with a black eye because he got that first right-hand sucker punch in.

Around that same time, I had my first encounter with the police. My friend Maurice and I went to visit our classmate, a white girl named Susan. Although we hadn't done anything, her mother called the police. Two white Plainfield officers chased us. Maurice got away. I got caught. They took me to the station and asked me what I was doing on that block. I told them that our classmate invited us to come by after school. I'm not sure what happened after that, but they told me to go home and not come around there again without an adult.

I was pissed that Maurice was faster than me. I knew that if I worked harder, I could beat Maurice or anyone else for that matter if I put my mind to track. I initially joined the track team for bragging rights, but then it became a passion and discipline that kept me on the straight and narrow. That incident with the police would be the first of many racial profiling incidents I endured throughout my adolescent and adult life.

My first track coach in middle school later became the first African American superintendent and mayor of Plainfield, Everett Lattimore. He was a very talented and extremely motivational coach who encouraged us to develop our skills. Our track team had great athletes who were setting records throughout the state—we were undefeated for several years. You had to bring your "A" game to have a chance at winning. My competitive nature was a key factor, as it took a lot of effort to win. But if you lost, the jokes were plentiful.

# CHAPTER 3

# BLACK REBELLION

*"You will not be able to stay home, brother*
*You will not be able to plug in, turn on and cop out*
*You will not be able to lose yourself on skag*
*And skip out for beer during commercials*
*Because the revolution will not be televised..."*
**— Gil Scott Heron**

I continued running track in high school. At that time in the mid-sixties, Black Power was the rallying cry, and I was down for the cause. I had high grades but was unsure of my life's trajectory. My dad wanted me to accomplish more than he did and not serve in the military. Fortunately, I had a high draft number, so serving in the Vietnam War was not in my plans. I was never interested in joining the armed forces because of the contradiction in the military. There was still racism in the military and one of the main objectives is to suppress people of color throughout the world.

Around this time, I was more aware of my environment. President Johnson had signed the Civil Rights Act in the summer of 1964, and issues of race and discrimination were on the news and in the papers every day. Much like today. My mom was a huge Malcolm X fan, and daddy was a real Martin champion. I gravitated to Malcolm as a teenager and listened to many of his speeches on vinyl records. I grew a fro and felt this mental and spiritual shift which started my journey of self and cultural awareness; "Say it loud, I'm Black, and I'm Proud!" In February 1965, when Malcolm X was assassinated at an event for the Organization of Afro American Unity in Harlem, I was pretty devastated. I thought of joining the Nation, but after his death, that path was not an option.

**Black Fact:** 1965 Watts, California, was the first major 1960's rebellion, aka riot. The community was responding to police brutality. Detroit and Newark 1967 were also examples of how the community responded with massive rebellions to police brutality. The Plainfield rebellion occurred because of the very same issue, police violence on a Black man. And this issue has a long and tragic history and has been a significant factor in most rebellions. On May 30, 2020, I was present at the peaceful protests in memory of George Floyd in Newark, and I believe it is one of the most historic moments in the history of the country." RIP George Floyd.

Two days after the Newark riots, Plainfield and other towns saw Blacks rebel. At 13 years old, I literally had a front-row seat to the Plainfield riots. I was sitting in an orange Volkswagen Beetle on Liberty Street with my soon to be brother-in-law, Ormie. It was the first time I saw military tanks that looked so powerful and frightening. The tanks were lined up in battle formation. Men in full tactical gear kicked in doors and smashed windows. I watched buildings set on fire. People were running with guns and shooting.

"Ormie, man, we have to get out of here," I kept screaming.

"No man, we have to stay and watch. We have to be able to tell our own story."

I thought he was crazy. We were sitting in this little car with nothing to protect us from the chaos. I did not understand why a riot or rebellion was taking place, but I knew it was a historic moment. For the next few days, Army tanks were going up and down the streets.

The impact was profound as a teenager trying to figure out who I was as a young Black man in a world where I witnessed a significant moment in history. Fear was the main thing during the riots. Mom and daddy warned us to stay away from the windows. Fortunately, we lived on the east end of Plainfield, the opposite side of town where the riots took place.

After the riots, the atmosphere quickly changed. I didn't understand this at the time. But in retrospect, as it pertains to the persistent issue of police brutality, school, and housing segregation, Plainfield, like many places, has become a predominant city of color.

*"We cannot think of being acceptable to others until we have first proven acceptable to ourselves."*
***— Malcolm X***

During that time in our culture, we were influenced by The Last Poets, Dick Gregory, The Black Panthers, and The Nation of Islam were instrumental in shaping current events. The greatest, Muhammad Ali, was also a major motivator. I recall in 1967 when a grand jury indicted Muhammad Ali for refusing to be inducted into the armed forces. Ali is famously quoted as saying, "I ain't got no quarrel with them, Viet Cong."

As a track and field athlete, another huge motivator for me to forge a path for my people was Tommie Smith and John Carlos' protest of the 1968 Olympics. The iconic image of two Black athletes with their fists raised on the Olympic podium impacted me to the core. Their powerful symbol of black power was a testament to the Civil Rights Movement at large.

Many of my peers were also on this cultural and political awakening journey. Today, Gen X and Millennials call it staying "woke." Back then, I had friends in the Black Panther Party, while others joined the Nation of Islam. The cultural mix and influences manifested in many ways in our style of dress and diet. I had already been following some customs of the Nation, and I stopped eating pork. I ultimately became a vegetarian, although I eat fish and limited shellfish. I began educating myself about our great African ancestors, and I was hungry to learn and do more for my people.

# CHAPTER 4

# MOTIVATION

*"Men can starve from a lack of self-realization as much as they can from a lack of bread."*
— **Richard Wright**

I had a great Black history teacher at Plainfield High School, Mr. Robinson. He was very knowledgeable and popular with all of the students. He challenged me to dig deeper than the narrative in the history books. Mr. Robinson's class reinforced the value of education in general and learning about the importance of my ancestors. Many of the students were very proud to be in his class. We wore fro's and talked about current events. What was also great about this class is that we discussed the Black music of the time. My classmates and I vibed to Marvin Gaye, Curtis Mayfield, The Temptations, Nina Simone, Sam Cooke, and Donnie Hathaway, among others. All of these great artists contributed to our understanding of our "blackness" and inspired us to learn more.

Classes like Mr. Robinson's and other lessons shaped my understanding of racism and society and my parenting approach. There is value in attending multiracial (ethnic) schools. It can help to clarify that we are as smart and talented as all other groups. There is also the real possibility of discrimination and not receiving the needed support and encouragement. The education I received in Plainfield prepared me to go to college. I didn't feel unprepared or inadequate. I did well academically but faced many challenges behaviorally. Attending Plainfield High School was very helpful when I later attended Rutgers because, at the time, there were very few African American students enrolled.

## On the Right Track

*"One important key to success is self-confidence. An important key to self-confidence is preparation.*

**— Arthur Ashe**

In high school, it was a time for teenagers to experiment with drugs. Many of my peers were trying out various drugs and alcohol on school grounds and at the good old-fashioned house parties. Indeed folks were trying to get higher and higher. I never had a desire to smoke. Daddy smoked Marlboro 100's. Sometimes two or three packs a day. From an early age, I hated smoke. Some of my friends liked to snort cocaine, use heroin, mescaline, and smoke weed. I remember a few kids cut school and were getting high in the garage with the door closed. They kept the car running, and a girl died from carbon monoxide poison. I was not involved with drugs, but I took risks like riding around in cars with dudes who had no license nor insurance. I also played stealing games with my buddies to see who could steal the most from local grocery stores. Most of the time, I grabbed a bunch of snacks like Hostess Twinkies and Wise Onion and Garlic Potato Chips.

Two of my friends Michael and David were serious about the Black Panthers. They were arrested and accused of killing a cop. Visiting

Michael and David would be the first of many visits to see someone in jail. They were eventually acquitted, which reinforced their work in the party. The Creator smiled upon me with a great friend named Bruce, who was on the track team. We made a pact not to get caught up in the "get high" and criminal activities. Fortunately, for us, it worked. Running track helped me stay out of trouble and not get suspended from school. Track provided a discipline that is still part of my life today. Back in high school, we had to do one hundred sit-ups, one hundred push-ups, and run two miles before we got to school. Today, I still do 50-85 push-ups and sit-ups five days a week.

My high school track coach, Ron Upperman, was also a great motivator. I could still hear him say, "C'ome on Davis!" He was very encouraging and believed I could accomplish more. I set a goal of running in the Penn Relays before high school graduation in 1972. My sister Jean took me to the Penn relays when I was in middle school. I'm not sure exactly why I was there, but it inspired me. In 1971, during my junior year, our team entered the 1600 meter relay, and I was the leadoff guy. We placed second. I still have my medal front and center on the shelf in my family room. That track meet was the only time my mom came to see me run, which was a blessing and also a lesson. When I became a parent, I decided that I would participate in all of my children's activities.

**Detour Ahead**

*"There is no better than adversity. Every defeat, every heartbreak, every loss, contains its own seed, its own lesson on how to improve your performance next time."*

**— Malcolm X**

I was working hard on running track and wanted to run a quarter-mile in 49 seconds. That never happened. Our family split in 1970, and my mother decided to sell our house and move to rural southern New Jersey, Williamstown, where her mother lived. This was during my junior year.

Mom enrolled me in high school in Williamstown. I thought this was the most backward place on Earth. I often cut school. The curriculum was leap years behind Plainfield. I made honor roll without much effort. The truant officer would come to my house, and I'd answer the door. He would say, "Man, you are the only one on the list on the honor roll! You've got to get your behind in the school building."

I hated Williamstown but quickly fell in love with Deidre, a Preacher's Kid (PK). During my senior year, my first child, a daughter, Monifa, was born. Her name means "I am the fortunate one," in African. A healthy child is definitely a blessing, but Deidre and my situation created a lot of drama. I had intended to go to college, and my parents were strongly urging me to get married and give my daughter the family name. They also encouraged me to get a job at the post office. Although it may sound selfish, I knew there was more for my life than settling for a job. I saw myself working for the United Nations or on an international level on behalf of my African brothers and sisters.

I knew I had to support Diedre and our daughter, so on weekends, I worked as a custodian at K-Mart mopping floors. This was an extremely complicated time in my life. Deidre's parents were religious, and my parents did not raise us with a religious background. I realized that whatever decision I made, everyone connected to me would not be happy. I ultimately decided to go to Rutgers, which was also close to Plainfield. My parents were disappointed in me not choosing to marry, but they were happy that I had chosen a solid foundation for my life's path. I felt a sting from my dad because I did not follow his example on the importance of raising your children.

In retrospect, the magnitude of this choice cannot be overstated. Making these difficult choices at an early age certainly prepared me for difficult future decisions. I was faced with a significant decision for the second time, and I had just turned 18. The first was to go back to Plainfield and live with my dad to run track, and the second was to attend Rutgers (RU). Even though I was leaving, I wanted to have a relationship with my daughter, Monifa. I saw her on weekends and often called. Since Deidre was a PK, her family wanted us to marry and for me to get a job at the post office, just like my parents wanted. I had done several manual labor jobs as a young person, and I knew that was not the life for me.

In the first year, I did not date. The second year, I fell in love with a young lady who complicated things with Deidre, who believed that once I graduated from RU, we would marry. Over time, my contact with Deidre and Monifa dwindled. When Monifa turned five, I stopped by her mother's house, and she informed me that Deidre had gotten married and moved to Pennsylvania. Her mother gave me the number. I called one day and left a congratulatory message and told her that if she needed anything to give me a call. Instead of a call from Deidre or Monifa, I got a call from Deidre's irate husband, who cursed me out and told me never to call his house again. I was shocked and disappointed. I reached out to Deidre another time to make sure she had my contact information.

Fast forward years later in 1990, I received a call from Monifa. I was shocked. I had visited her grandmother a few months prior and mentioned that I was no longer at RU, but I had accepted a position at NYU as an Assistant Director. Monifa found me in the staff directory and called my direct line. We talked over a few things, and she informed me that she wanted to go to NYU. At that time, she never mentioned to her mother, Diedre, that she contacted me. I told her that it was best to talk to her mother. I spoke to Diedre, and we cleared the air. I was looking forward to starting a new relationship with my daughter and the Crew.

When Monifa turned 18, she came to live with my children and me. She bonded with her siblings right away. When we walked around the city, I knew she was not ready to live in the Big Apple. The culture shock from southern Pennsylvania to New York City was too drastic. She toughed it out for a few months, and later I got her into Rutgers where she did well. During that time, she informed me of some very traumatic experiences in her childhood. I was surprised and felt guilty about her pain. Monifa and I went to counseling together. Sadly, she has not gotten over the fact that I was not there for her as a child. She ended all communication with me. It hurts deeply, and I hope we can re-establish a relationship again. As parents, we make mistakes. I cannot go back and change the decisions I made as my younger self. All I can do is love Monifa and be open and available to help if needed.

The moving back and forth within the state during high school helped shape my parenting style. I wanted to limit choices and moves that would interrupt my Crew's education and living situation. Although Sekou and Toussaint did leave Piscataway High School to attend Rutgers Prep, it was a collaborative decision. Sometimes parents may not realize the impact these changes have on their children.

My mom had her first child in Williamstown, and she was not married. Like Mom, my first child was born in Williamstown, and I was not married. Sometimes, however unwittingly, children repeat or follow the examples of their parents. This lesson was one that I would later emphasize with my Crew. Teenage parenting was a generational problem that the Davis family had to break.

# CHAPTER 5

# BROTHER BLACK

*"Courage is the most important of all the virtues because, without courage, you can't practice any other virtue consistently. You can practice any virtue erratically, but nothing consistently without courage. "*

**— Dr. Maya Angelou**

I was determined to go to college and graduate. As I mentioned, my two older sisters went to college and did not finish. They both married at young ages. Marriage was not in my scope. I was not prepared for marriage, but I cared for Deidre and loved my daughter very much. I wanted to figure out a way to make this work. I was happy to have a child who was healthy with a spunky, interactive personality. Then I'd feel guilty about our situation and the fact that I did not marry her mother. This was a significant paradox; I have a nice lady, a healthy child, no intention to marry and catching heat from both families.

I was eager to get my college life started. I had already been partying on the RU campus on the weekends when I was in Plainfield, so my college life became official. There was a community group in Plainfield that helped students with college admissions and financial aid applications. Thankfully, I qualified for the Educational Opportunity Fund (EOF) and ended up living on the College Avenue Campus of RU in the Clothier Dorm.

Attending college classes was quite surprising at first. In high school, I was surrounded by Black students, and I hung out at the RU parties on weekends with Blacks. I was not expecting my classes to be predominantly white. In a few classes, I was the only Black student. This was definitely a factor in deciding to become an Africana Studies major.

When I set foot on Rutgers campus as a freshman, I was in full "Black Power" mode. I was immediately given the nickname "Brother Black" by my peers because my conversation revolved around the plight of the Black student and Black people in general. I helped set up The Black Student Congress and worked with different organizations to plan for Black History Month and other inclusive events. In my second and third year, I was a lot more active on campus and dating. I fell in love with a woman named Brenda, whom everyone called *Ebony Woman* after the song by Billy Paul. She was pretty, tall, petite, with a beautiful fro. I was head over heels for her until I found out she was cheating on me. Brenda was the first woman to break my heart. Who knows, maybe that was my karma for breaking Diedre's heart.

I decided to major in Africana Studies despite my family and friends who opposed my choice. I enjoyed the professors and the material. I grew intellectually as the material we studied and debated expanded my knowledge. Some of my favorite professors were Dr. Bethel, Dr. Van Sertima, and Dr. Carter. During that time, I had no idea that I would one day have the privilege of teaching. Hopefully, I have been able to inspire the students in my classes, similar to how my early professors motivated me. I was also active in the Students for Afro American Society (SAS), Blacks United to Save Themselves (BUST), Black Voice, and the African Student Congress. Campus life allowed me to learn more about myself, history, and to develop my leadership skills. I was selected as President of SAS and played a key role in campus protests and events. These experiences were critical to shaping my career and life.

In my Junior year, I helped set up the Black Student Congress and had two impactful years as the President of the SAS. RU was a racist campus with a horrible retention rate of Black students and had very few Black faculty. During a RU basketball game broadcast on State TV, we stopped the game to protest the blatant discrimination and racist treatment of Blacks. We read our list of demands, including more Black faculty, staff, students, and more support services. We also had other significant protests in the library and held several demonstrations in front of the President of RU's house. Sadly, the university administration would make promises, but no significant changes were made.

I was grateful to be in a leadership position to participate in these historical events. I wrote articles for the Black Voice Newspaper, and they posted a picture of me in my senior year. Later, I was part of a Rutgers board of governors meeting regarding anti-apartheid. At that time, Lisa Williamson, aka Sista Souljah, was a student, so I got a chance to work with her in campus protest activities.

In addition to my classes and extracurricular activities, I also worked in various offices on campus. At that time, Dean Clark was the only African American in the Dean of Students' office. He was a kind and caring person who helped many students navigate the maze of life at RU. Some folks did not appreciate his calm demeanor, especially since this was a period of marching, protesting, and being militant.

I also served as a student recruiter in the admissions office. My role was to attend recruitment events and offer a student perspective. Two of my mentors, Don Phifer and Willie Hamm, were instrumental in helping me to understand the admissions process. In addition, they were instrumental in my hiring at RU Camden. My mentors and I were kindred spirits. I enjoyed being with them and others as they gave the president "hell" regarding the lack of students, faculty, and staff of color.

RU was a great foundation for my life's purpose and career. I was enriched by many of my classmates who were intelligent, courageous, and committed to community uplift. Some attended graduate school; others went to law or medical school. There were a few who went to work after graduation. One of the challenges of attending a predominantly white institution is that after graduation, you lose contact with "folks." Sadly my classmates rarely returned for homecoming or other campus events. We did not have the luxury of cell phones and social media to stay in touch like college students today.

In May 1976, when I graduated from RU, it was a beautiful day. My parents, sisters, and brothers, and my track buddy, Bruce, were in attendance. Bruce and I had planned to make a cross country trip that summer, but he fell in love and changed his mind. I hadn't been looking for work and was unemployed for several months.

My first professional job was coincidentally at RU Camden as an Admissions Counselor. The director that hired me left and was replaced by an overzealous person whom I clashed with often. Soon after, I was transferred to RU's New Brunswick campus. Despite the office challenges, I completed my Master's Degree in Education while working full-time in New Brunswick.

At that time, I met Lennox Hinds. He was a lawyer and taught criminal justice. He invited me to take part in an anti-apartheid movement. I had already moved all of my belongings to New York by myself. I had a silent roommate, a car, a van, and a nice apartment. I was now working for the RU Newark campus and commuting from New York every day. I had also traveled outside the country, including Kenya. I set my sights on a future position at the United Nations after working on my first anti-apartheid conference. I'm not sure why Lennox Hinds invited me, but I am glad he did. It was my first experience working on Pan-Africanism and turned out to be a seminal event in my life.

## *Reflections: UN Planning Meeting to End Apartheid*

July 18th, 1981

777 United Nations Plaza,

I'm in a meeting planning the 1st US national conference in opposition to apartheid. I was invited by Lennox Hinds, a faculty member at Rutgers who is also a lawyer and held a leadership position in the International Lawyers Guild. My role was to help organize youth and folks who advocate for nationalism; I met one of many mentors Elombe Brath via this effort.

The conference is held at Riverside Church with hundreds in attendance. The conference would catalyze many years of anti-apartheid efforts throughout the country and the world.

Conference in Solidarity with the Liberation Struggles of the Peoples of Southern Africa

Riverside Church, New York City

Guest Speaker Hon. Ronald V. Dellums,

President of the Preparatory Committee Lennox S. Hinds, Esq., Chair of the Preparatory Committee Secretariat.

# PART II
# Fatherhood

*"Children are one of the greatest rewards in life, and also the greatest challenge."*
**— Bill Davis**

# CHAPTER 6

# SOMETHING IN COMMON

*"You—light the way, you brighten up my day*
*You make me want to stay,*
*I guess you know that I'm in love with you*
*It's true, you changed my point of view..."*
***— Earth Wind and Fire, "You"***

In the winter of 1981, I was having dinner and drinks at "The Cellar" with good friends Mary Davis and Vince Henry. Both Mary and Vince were established artists in the music industry. Mary sang backup for Luther Vandross, Whitney Houston, David Bowie, and Mariah Carey. Vince was on the jazz scene working with Jonathan Butler, and the group Bring in the Noise. As dinner was coming to a close, a beautiful woman walked up to our table to speak to Mary. Her name was Marilyn, and she was Mary's roommate. Marilyn talked briefly and mentioned she was a model. Mary recognized the attraction and made a formal introduction. Marilyn and I started dating a short time later.

I was living on 95th Street and Columbus Avenue in an Upper West Side apartment. Marilyn and I hit it off early. We both were vegetarians and were into fitness and exercise. One of the things that she said attracted her to me was that I was into activism, and did not care about modeling or fashion like most of the people she had met in New York. She was from Milwaukee and moved to New York to become a model.

She had family in New Jersey who was connected to Mary, so Mary helped her find her way. Marilyn was doing well and had several shoots in the works. One day my roommate saw her in GQ Magazine.

"Hey man, yo ain't that your woman?"

"Yeah," I replied nonchalantly.

"Do you know what that means? She's the only Black person in the magazine! They rarely include Black models. She's definitely going to be famous!"

"Well, that's great for her if that's what she wants," I responded.

Marilyn's father's origins are in Haiti, but her parents owned a grocery store in Milwaukee. Her father was a quiet man, while her mother and aunt were strong matriarchs. Marilyn was a virgin when we met. We discussed contraception, and both agreed that we wanted to do things as naturally as possible, so she was not on the pill. I believed she was using a diaphragm and planned to get an IUD. Six months later, she was pregnant. I wanted to do the right thing this time around, so we were married within a year. Ironically, our families met for the first time at the wedding. I remember my sister commenting on Marilyn's dad being handsome.

The wedding took place at the International House in New York on Riverside Drive. It was a beautiful hall with an African wedding theme. Marilyn was not very politically cultural, but African interests and influence were significant to me, and she was open to learning more. Before the wedding, she wanted to share something with me that she never told anyone.

"I am going to say something that I hope will not make you uncomfortable."

"Go ahead. I can handle it." I reassured her.

"I have anxiety. I'm seeing a therapist, and I have been for a while."

I was surprised, but then shrugged it off. "OK, cool with me. As long as you are doing what you need to do." I had no idea the extent of Marilyn's mental illness and did not do my due diligence. Many women that I had dated previously had stories of early molestation or other trauma, so this was different, yet manageable, I told myself. Early on, Marilyn appeared happy, healthy, and confident in her ability to accomplish her lofty goals of being a world-class model.

Amid this new revelation, Marilyn and I took childbirth classes with a midwife three days a week. We were excited about the new addition to our family, but we also knew it would mean changes and sacrifices to our careers. When I moved to New York, I was invited by Lennox Hinds to the UN for an apartheid planning meeting. I hoped to get a job at the UN and spend my life traveling the world. Marilyn was in the prime of her modeling career. Having a child would require a significant change for her as well. In addition to her getting back into shape for the industry and travel, we would have to figure out childcare arrangements.

More importantly, I could not have a wife and child in the shared apartment with my roommate, so I had to find us a place to live. It made sense to move to New Jersey since I was working at RU as an academic advisor. In the back of my mind, I still had aspirations of attaining a UN job. I convinced myself that it would happen in due time, but for now, I had to focus on being Baba the right way—in a nuclear family to make mom and daddy proud.

# CHAPTER 7

# SEKOU

*"It is better to build strong children than to repair broken men."*
**— Frederick Douglass**

I was in the delivery room with a video camera in hand for the births of all four of the Crew. On October 13, 1982, Sekou Keita Babatunde made his debut. Sekou means "one who fights for just causes," Keita, "one who worships," and Babatunde, "father is reborn." He was born at Roosevelt St. Luke's Hospital on West 59th Street. The midwife was excellent. She used warm oils and massage. It was an awesome experience to see a new life enter the world. I can still see the extraordinary moment of Sekou's head sprouting, followed by his full body. The only cutting was when I cut the umbilical cord. They set it up perfectly, so it is hard to miss!

I'm sure my children's names didn't follow the traditional way names are chosen, but I did honor the tradition with my own flavor. I had the privilege to meet Sekou Toure, the former President of Guinea. A friend and mentor, the late Brother Elombe Brath invited me to go with him to the airport to greet the President. I must admit it was a great surprise to see Brother Elombe and President Sekou embrace like old friends.

There was also another brother named Sekou Sundiata, a talented poet and spoken word artist. He was a member of a group called "Are and Be." Their most popular song was "How You Gonna Make the Black

Nation Rise," with Brother D. When Sekou was born, I was ecstatic. Like many fathers, I always wanted a son. The idea of a son to carry on your name and traditions was important. He was born on a Wednesday afternoon like me. He looked like me and was left-handed like me. Later, he would also be very devious like me. Again, I really admired the name Sekou and if I did not have the respect and admiration of my father, William Davis, Sr. I would have changed my name to Sekou.

When Sekou came home from the hospital, we were living in New York. Actually, the day he was born, they towed my car for parking on the wrong side of the street, and we had to take a cab to the hospital. Marilyn spent two days in the hospital. We did not have a nursery set up as we were planning to move to Plainfield, New Jersey. I purchased a foreclosed home for $30,000. My father and I painted and got the house in order.

The move to Plainfield was drastic for Marilyn. Not only was she dealing with postpartum depression, she felt isolated in a town where she knew no one. At the time, she did not have a driver's license, so she couldn't even venture to the store or the park. When I left for work in the morning, Marilyn and Sekou were in bed. When I returned in the evening, they were still in bed. I tried to do my part and alleviate her responsibilities as soon as I got home. I handled the diaper duties and feeding. Marilyn was breastfeeding, so she pumped bottles to give herself a break. Some days she was anxious to get back to modeling, and other days she could not get out of bed. On the weekends, I took her for driving lessons, and she got her license a short while after that. Marilyn lost the weight and was in picture-perfect shape. She landed a feature in a parenting magazine with Sekou.

Two years later, in 1984, there was an opportunity to move into a beautiful home in Newark. My family thought I was crazy, leaving Plainfield to go to Newark until they saw our house. I purchased a brick, two-family home with two bedrooms and separate utilities. Marilyn's friends, Mary and Vince, lived on the first floor and we lived on the second. Newark offered more cultural awareness programs for our family, so it was the right move at the right time.

**Dat Dere**

*Hey daddy, what's that there?*
*And what's that doing there?*
*Hey daddy, up here! Daddy, hey look at that over there!*
*And what's that doing there?*
*And where they going there?*
*And daddy, can I have that big elephant over there?...*
**— Oscar Brown, Jr.**

Sekou was on target in his toddler years and was walking and talking before his first birthday. He displayed academic and artistic gifts at an early age. As a parent, I always hoped that my children would be healthy and have a unique talent, whether artistic, academic, or athletic. Witnessing my children's development of these talents was exciting, yet I had to be mindful to keep my balance through the process. Sekou was a student at the Chad School, an Afrocentric school in Newark. The school was run by Brother Pat, a no-nonsense administrator who kept the kids in line and expanded their minds. The expectations to succeed were very high, and the school also allowed the students the freedom of creative expression. For their talent show, he formed a singing and dancing group with his friends to perform Bobby Brown's "Every Little Step." This was his first time on stage in front of a crowd, and he enjoyed having the ability to entertain others through song.

By kindergarten, he was counting to 100 and playing the keyboard. At seven years old, he could name all 50 states and their capitals from a blank map. He wasn't the only student in his class who was multi-talented. Several others also made their parents proud. I recall one of the things Sekou did not like about the Chad school was that they had to wear green and gold uniforms, which represented the natural resources in Africa. Sekou's gifts were a powerful omen of what was on the horizon. He was the most curious of the Crew and asked questions nonstop. I dedicated Oscar Brown Jr.'s, *Dat Dere* to Sekou, for his never-ending imagination, creativity, and inquisitiveness.

I know many parents who have been confronted by their children and others, asking, "Who is your favorite child?" I imagine we all have the same response, "I don't have a favorite; I love all of my children equally." Although my children never said Sekou was my favorite, I honestly believe they may have felt it because he was a triple threat at such a young age: smart, artistic, and athletic. A role model for Sekou and all of the Crew was Paul Robeson, a literal and figurative giant Rutgers alum and world citizen. His accomplishments were truly incredible, especially given the times. Robeson graduated Phi Beta Kappa and was the only African American student. He earned 17 letters and was a two-time All American football player. Robeson became the most recognized person in the world for his activism and work as an artist on the stage.

To round out the triple threat was Sekou's athleticism. He was enrolled in a gymnastics program called 'Flip City,' which helped

African American and Latino children learn flips and other gymnastic moves. While living in Newark, it was essential to keep the Crew involved in extracurricular activities. The first time Sekou walked into the YMCA gym, he was mesmerized. Seeing kids that looked like him doing backflips gave him the confidence that if he practiced, he could do it too.

They all started at the beginner level, "Baby Chick," and moved up to become a "Sparrow." He was determined to fly like a sparrow one day. At age eight, Sekou was placed on the travel team. There was a national competition in Baton Rouge, where he placed third because he kept landing over the flip line. Being on a national stage was intimidating. While he practiced for countless hours, his nerves got the best of him. His team performed at various events, and he even had a chance to perform at the New Jersey Nets game at the Meadowlands Arena. There were thousands of people in attendance, and Sekou and all the team members did their amazing acrobatic routine. Those early accomplishments, among others, were an indication of what he could accomplish in the future.

It was not until we moved to Piscataway in 1992 when Sekou started in a new school, he began having academic problems as a result of hanging with knuckleheads. This was a difficult time for him for two reasons: 1) It was a move away from his best friend and the programs he enjoyed, and 2) It was the first time his mom was not moving with us. Being rebellious was a way of acting out his anger and disappointment that he did not have his mother at home.

When I enrolled Sekou in Arbor School, I met the principal and explained that Sekou was on the honor roll and that my expectation was for his scholarly achievement to continue. The principal was skeptical and mentioned that while he hoped this would happen, he nor I should be surprised if it didn't. He explained that other students had enrolled from similar schools and had a difficult adjustment. I said that Sekou had been in various settings, including integrated ones, and always excelled. I was determined to make sure that the principal's skepticism would not deter his progress. Sekou made the honor roll as he had done so before and was promoted to the fifth grade. This would prove to be a challenging year behaviorally.

Jawanza Kunjufu wrote a book, *Countering the Conspiracy to Destroy Black Boys*, where he describes the fourth-grade failure syndrome. His position is that African American boys do as well as all children through the fourth grade when they start to get disinterested in school. In Sekou's case, his academic progress was on track, but he was distracted. We were fortunate that his teacher, Ms. Kelly, was a very talented and experienced African American woman who advocated for our children and believed in teacher and parent communication. We agreed to speak weekly to assess if Sekou had stayed on task. If he was on task, he could have the privilege of television and video games. If he was off task, those privileges were taken away.

I immediately saw how my children were willing to test the boundaries I had set to see if I was going to stick to my decision. I knew that if I did not reinforce my position on these types of issues, I would face even more difficult issues in the future. There was also the peer reinforcement of the other siblings. To ensure that the no TV or video game rules were followed, I would take the remote controllers and disconnect the cable box so none of the children could have access to these privileges. Clearly, this was unfair to the rest of the Crew, but my actions made it clear to Sekou that he needed to get on track.

At one point, Ms. Kelly told me of a stereotypical racist description of Sekou as told to her by a white staff member. Sekou was in the after school program. One of the staff complained to Ms. Kelly, saying, "Sekou is a really terrible kid. He plays too rough, and takes the games seriously."

"Really? I'm surprised to hear this. Sekou is doing very well academically and is on the honor roll."

The man's face dropped. The issue of stereotyping and having low expectations for African American children, especially boys, manifests in many ways. I advised Sekou that as a Black male, white people will be afraid of you. I have been racially profiled more times than I can count as a Black male with dreads. I always wanted my kids to be prepared for this kind of reality. My interactions with Sekou's teacher and principal reinforce the need for parents to stay in tune, continuously encourage our children, and help them understand that they have to be mindful of how they present themselves in public.

The ironic thing about Sekou in the middle school years was that he was on the honor roll, but he was always acting up. One time he and his friends were riding bikes and went to an office park that was under construction. They threw rocks and broke out the windows. I already had several conversations with Sekou that if the police come, do not run, "Whatever happens, we will handle it. Do what they say and wait until I get there!" Someone called the police. When the cops showed up, his friends rode away like lightning. Sekou waited for the police to approach. I was happy that he followed my direction, but I was clearly irritated that he was throwing rocks at a building! The police were cordial, and nothing further came after that incident—except a long punishment and no privileges for Sekou.

## Young, Gifted, and Black

Sekou attended Quibbletown Middle School and continued in the music program he started in elementary school. All fifth-grade students selected an instrument to learn during band class. He chose to play drums, an instrument that immediately connected with him, and ultimately shaped his future. By seventh grade, his music teacher said to me, "he just has it!" Sekou continued to do well academically while playing pop warner football, playing two positions: running back and a defensive back. He made a few touchdowns and was viewed as one of the more talented players. Pop Warner football was a family affair. Both Sekou and Toussaint played football, Imani and Naeemah were cheerleaders, and I was the first Black play-by-play announcer the area had ever had. By this time, Sekou also started playing basketball, which would eventually become his favorite sport. In seventh grade, he had an altercation with a white kid, and punches were thrown. Sekou was suspended longer than the other kid. This gave him another personal experience that African American boys are always seen as a threat.

In eighth grade, Sekou was expected to continue to play both offensive and defensive back, but he had decided that he only wanted to play basketball. When we attended the pop warner practices, many parents and children encouraged him to play, but he stayed firm and switched to basketball. I followed my parent's philosophy of "no quitting!" If you joined a team, you had to complete the whole season. I didn't push football at the time because his plate was already full with Boy Scouts as well.

Eighth grade was another pivotal lesson for Sekou. His friend Hal started drumming with Sekou in fifth grade. Through the first couple of years, Sekou's natural ability to pick up on drum rhythms made him the top choice for band solos. Hal was determined to work harder and started taking private drum lessons. By their eighth grade year, Hal was now as talented as Sekou. That incident reinforced my message to my Crew that people who are willing to work hard or harder will catch or pass people with natural talent, but don't make an effort.

Sekou refocused his energy with a harder work ethic after seeing what it takes to get to the next level—Piscataway High School drumline. During an assembly for the eighth-graders, the high school marching band presented for the incoming freshman. Sekou was in awe at their abilities, especially the quad drums. He concluded middle school on the honor roll, excelled in music, and sports. He was now ready for the next big step—high school.

## The Chiefs

Sekou's transition to Piscataway High School went very well. He took the academic track and prepared to participate in sports and music programs. The Piscataway music program was well developed with the intention of students participating in either high school marching band or other musical ensembles. Sekou was in the high school band drumline and represented The Chiefs very well. The band practices were intense. They practiced as much as the sports teams. The summertime commitment involved three-hour daily practices as the students learned not only the musical component but also the marching steps. For two weeks in August, Sekou left for band camp where the entire band would spend morning, noon, and night rehearsing for the upcoming season.

The band leader had a strong commitment to excellence and reinforced Sekou's participation. Fortunately, since he had already switched to basketball, there was no conflict with sports. The band participated in local and regional competitions and had an excellent reputation. They also traveled to various places for competitions around the country. Another benefit of the band was that many of the students were also talented academically. Hence, being in honor classes or on the honor roll was not unusual, and he was in his zone.

I think one of the many conflicts African American families face is the idea that to be smart is to "act white." This thought process is a profound disrespect of our history, given the significant contributions of great Black intellectuals. However, far too many Black children will say in the parlance of the neighborhood, "you think you all that!" Overcoming this form of "brainiac" peer pressure is one of the greatest challenges adolescents face. As parents, we must use multiple strategies to help our children to combat that stereotypical pressure.

During the summer between his freshman and sophomore year in high school, Sekou's friend James introduced him to the DJ business. This new gig was certainly in alignment with his love for music and added to his popularity. There were many parties, and the business did well. One of their most successful endeavors was when they rented out the Middlesex County College gymnasium to throw a high school party. Over one thousand students attended the party, and it was the most talked about event of the school year.

On the other hand, one of our funniest family stories sprung as a result of Sekou's DJ efforts. Someone told Sekou that Wu-Tang Clan was going to be in a nearby park, and they needed a DJ. I explained to him that this story doesn't make any sense. I took him to the park. We waited in the park for a couple of hours with no sign that Wu-Tang Clan was coming. Sekou was steadfast that the performance would happen.

After a while, we saw a limo, and several other cars pull up. Sekou was really excited thinking Wu-Tang had finally arrived. It turned out to be a wedding party! I laughed so hard it hurt. Just thinking about it now still makes me crack up.

Of the four children in the Davis crew, Sekou always pushed the limits to my parenting. He had a summer job working in the cafeteria at Johnson & Johnson. The rule was that you could keep half of your money, and the other half goes into your savings account. I had just pulled in from work, and I saw Sekou getting out of a taxi in front of our house. He had taken a taxi round trip to hang out with a girl on the other side of town. I was furious that he thought he could just catch a cab to a girl's house. "Are you out of your damned mind?" I questioned. Of course, he believed it was no big deal because it was "his money!"

I recall another incident when I was laying down resting. I heard the front door open and close. The other three kids were watching TV. Then I heard Sekou telling his siblings that he was riding around in a car with a kid named Trey. Sekou was well aware that Trey had no license nor insurance. All of a sudden, I came up from behind out of the darkness. I was fired up. I grabbed Sekou and held him tight. The other kids thought I was going to hurt him. Again, Sekou challenged every parenting ideal known to man. Fortunately, the rest of the Crew saw how much hell Sekou caught; they did not want any parts of it! Not to say that they did not make mistakes or act out, it's just that they did not get caught. Sekou got caught a lot. I was serious about keeping all of them on track. I emphasized that there could be hell at home or hell on the streets, but if you take the hell on the streets route, they have places to put you. Sekou and his siblings clearly needed to respect a safe and relatively drama-free space at home.

Sekou transferred to Rutgers Prep for his junior and senior years. The school had an excellent academic reputation but was marginal in sports. At Piscataway High School, Sekou excelled in both. We discussed that there would be many students from affluent families and that access to drugs and alcohol would be easy. He responded that many students he knew at Piscataway High School were already involved in this lifestyle, so he was confident that he could stay on track at Rutgers Prep. He was the second-best player on the basketball team during his junior year. By senior year, he was the best. He was selected to the all-state team for prep schools. He was also awarded a presidential scholarship to attend Hampton University, where James, his friend and music partner, had enrolled a year before.

During his first year at Hampton, Sekou fully immersed himself into the HBCU lifestyle. His network not only extended on campus but also grew within the music business. By winter break his freshman year, Sekou had attracted the attention of music managers who helped propel his work to the next level and earned him his first production placement. Sekou shared with me the excitement as cars would ride by blasting his latest song from their vehicles. He would eventually earn a gold record for his work with the rap artist Cassidy on his major-label debut.

All of this newfound success carried into Sekou's sophomore year when Sekou and his business partners decided it was time to dedicate their efforts full-time to music. The plan was to put their Hampton education to use in the real world. Sekou and his team wrote out a business plan which attracted an investor offering $50,000 as seed money into their new company, The I.N. Crowd, LLC. The conversation surrounding his ultimate decision to drop out of Hampton was one of the great paradoxes for me. As a lifelong educator, I instilled in my Crew the importance of higher learning from early on. What example was I setting if I allowed my oldest son to leave college early? One the other hand, this was his dream, and I wanted to support his passion in any way possible. I also did not want my son to live with the regret of not following his heart and taking a chance to do what he loved. I gave Sekou my blessing, and he moved back to New Jersey with his partners to begin their entrepreneurial pursuits.

Sekou now had a new apartment, music studio, and opportunities. The first few years of this venture seemed to be successful. Yet the unpredictability of the music business concerned me that Sekou's ability to care for himself long-term would be difficult. Additionally, the unhealthy nature of the studio setting encouraged a lifestyle that I could not condone. This was the life that he chose, and at a certain point in time, I began to feel that I was actually enabling this behavior. It became clear that I needed to help Sekou shift his focus. In 2010, we set out a plan for Sekou to return to Rutgers and finish his degree. His graduation and employment offer in 2012 was a very proud moment for our family. Sekou would now work full-time while still pursuing his musical endeavors part-time. Burning the candle at both ends definitely took a toll on him. I believe it was Nia's birth that ultimately helped my son see it was time to slow down and live a life that will best support his new family. Sometimes the universe has a way of sending these profound messages to us at precisely the right time.

*Sekou toddler years.*

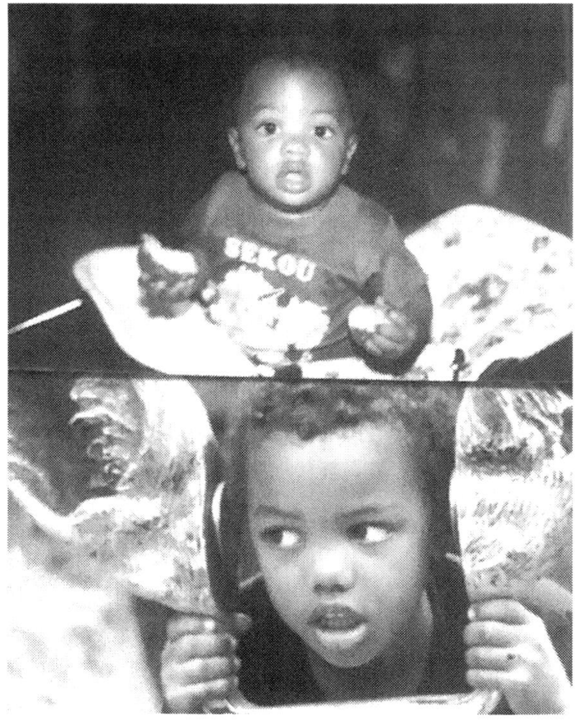

# CHAPTER 8

# TOUSSAINT

*"The single most important part of running and winning your own race –is recognizing that you are enough and that you are an original."*
**— Robert F. Smith**

Marilyn and I were on our first trip to Egypt with Dr. Ben. When we returned, Marilyn was pregnant. Toussaint Osiris was born early Sunday morning, November 18, 1984, at Saint Peters Hospital in New Brunswick. Toussaint was named in honor of one of the key leaders of the Haitian Revolution, Toussaint Louverture. As a general, Louverture was instrumental in the Haitian people's fight for freedom from slavery by the French.

***Rainbow Child***
*He was born on Sunday morning to carry on*
*Carry on*
*It was like a ray of sunshine come the dawn*
*Come the dawn*
*And I looked at him and smiled*
*When I realized this child*
*Had come into the world*
*To carry on*
*Carry on*
***— Angela Bofill***

At an early age, Toussaint would come into our bedroom and say, "the sun is shining," reflecting his sunny personality. He has large bright eyes, dark brown curly hair, and often described as a "pretty" baby. Some of his favorite things were giving and receiving hugs and playing wrestling to start the day.

Toussaint has become the "tallest tree" in our family forest. He grew fast, but it wasn't always that way. For the majority of his pre-adolescence and early teenage years, he was average height and very slight. This would undoubtedly impact both his confidence and desire to gain weight later in life. At times, it reminded me of my brother Kevin's desire to get stronger. Kevin always had a slight build, and he would lift weights like crazy to beef up.

## Scouts Honor

One of the activities my sons participated in was Boys Scouts. The troop was composed of Black boys with Black adult leadership. While it was no one's favorite activity, I think they liked the camaraderie it formed. Sekou was around 12 years old and Toussaint 10. We only participated for a couple of years, but it was fundamental in their development of being around positive Black male youth in something other than sports. One year, we all went on an overnight trip to Stokes Forest that had many funny, memorable moments. We stayed in cabins in the forest and a mouse was living behind the stove. All of the boys were trying to catch it. The scout leader pricked his finger, pretending the mouse had bitten him. Then, while two boys were trying to catch the mouse, I came behind one of the boys with a twisted napkin and pretended the mouse sneaked up on him. He jumped out of his skin! Later, he had a nightmare thinking the mouse was in his sleeping bag. Another memorable moment was in the middle of the night Toussaint had to go to the bathroom. He was afraid to go by himself, so he only made it out of the cabin and left a "load" near the door. The next morning the boys and scout leader assumed a bear had been there based on the output.

## Middle Child

Toussaint is smart and talented, although his abilities manifested later than his brother. Like me, Toussaint is a middle child, which was a challenge because there can be rivalry with both older and younger siblings. The irony in the sibling rivalry is that they care deeply for each other. When Toussaint was six, we visited a water park in Virginia, and Toussaint tried to go up the water slide. He slipped and cut his chin. The injury was bloody and required several stitches. Sekou was very sad and concerned. It was a memorable family moment. It took a long time for him to develop his athletic talent. Like Paul Robeson, who also had an older brother, Toussaint worked to find his place in the family, school, and community.

The issue of sibling rivalries is a huge challenge that many parents face, including me. I don't have any profound insight to offer, only to continuously reassure each child that you love them for who they are regardless of their talent. There were many times when the tensions between my sons were very intense. One time, when they were riding bikes, Toussaint fell. Instead of Sekou helping, he laughed at him. When they got home, Toussaint was so angry he threw a pen and just missed striking Sekou in the eye. There were a few lessons to be learned in this incident like check to see if someone is hurt, and if they are, exhibit some form of care.

During that time, I could not understand why Toussaint had so much more laundry than everyone else. I found out that he was wearing two or three T-Shirts. For a short time, I nicknamed him three shirts! Only much later did I realize that he felt self-conscious about how thin he was. Getting bigger and stronger is like a rite of passage for young boys. Maybe it's the male personality to compete. When correctly channeled, it can be healthy. But there are consequences as a challenge the younger sibling faces is how to get the older sibling to respect boundaries. Toussaint had to learn to get Sekou to limit his behavior, which didn't happen until they both grew apart. Toussaint needed to find his footing and confidence amongst his friends, which only happened when he wasn't in Sekou's shadow anymore.

## The Tallest Tree

As he continued to grow, I always felt he had trouble being in the shadow of his brother and coping with the emerging talent of his sisters. Throughout middle school, Toussaint maintained honor roll but was never a straight-A student like his sisters, nor was he multi-talented musically and athletically as his brother. His coping mechanism, more often than not, was through being approachable both in and out of the classroom, which at times hindered his success and got him into minor trouble. He stole cookies from the cafeteria and got into a few fights.

That, however, helped his popularity and confidence. After a tumultuous freshman year at Rutgers Prep, where he underperformed academically, he transferred back to Piscataway High School. It was at his neighborhood high school where he found his footing in and out of the classroom. This was the first time he wasn't in anyone's shadow, and I believe that helped him grow into his own person. It is also when he found his first love and best friends.

Going back to Piscataway High School rekindled his friendship with our neighbor Jarret Meyers. Though they knew each other in middle school, it wasn't until high school when the pair became inseparable. If Toussaint was not home, he was directly across the street with Jarret. He and Jarret would play basketball, football, and video games regularly. In addition to the special friendship he formed with Jarret, I believe he felt a special warmth in Jarret's mother, Liz. She filled a maternal void and would love him as a son. Liz would chide him when he wasn't doing as well as he could in the classroom. I knew he was in good hands when he was across the street with the Meyers'.

Toussaint and Jarret played on the high school basketball team together, and while they were more talented than most of the teams they played, the coaches had a hard time harnessing their collective gifts. Toussaint had grown to about 6'5" by his high school senior year. He was one of the better players on the high school basketball team and was thinking of playing in college. I encouraged him to consider an HBCU because he would get a quality education and be able to play. This was during the 2000-2001 season, and Hampton was one of seven 15th seeds to upset the 2nd seed in the Round of 64 of an NCAA Tournament, defeating Iowa State in the first round. Sekou had attended Hampton as a presidential scholar, but Toussaint was determined to set his own path and did not want to attend Hampton. Instead, he chose Rutgers, and I believe his girlfriend Ellie was a significant factor. At Rutgers, he started playing basketball and lifting weights. He gained 20-30 pounds, mainly muscle, and grew to 6' 6," which helped his athletic ability. He played recreational basketball, and one of his favorite moves was to dunk on somebody.

Toussaint's high school girlfriend, Ellie, was from a first-generation Filipino family. This was the first time our family experienced an interracial relationship. Ellie was attractive, smart, and very caring. Our family really liked her, particularly Imani and Naeemah, as they felt she was a good fit for him. However, it did not appear that Toussaint was received by her family the same way. They had probably been dating for eight or nine months before I even met her parents. After learning he was going to attend Rutgers, and he had his act together, Ellie's parents were more receptive and saw how much he cared for their daughter. They went to her senior prom together. Toussaint was very excited about how beautiful the evening was, although Ellie's parents did not permit them to attend any activities afterward. Ellie graduated a year before Toussaint and attended Rutgers. Despite a few challenges, they stayed together for several years.

Back in high school, math was a challenge for Toussaint. He decided to major in finance at Rutgers, even though math was always his weakest subject. Almost by accident, he ended up on Busch Campus, which unbeknownst to him, was where the engineering school was housed. To his credit, he made friends with students in the engineering school who assisted him in math. His friends from freshman dorm remained his friends throughout his four years at Rutgers even though they all had different disciplines. Toussaint and Ellie were able to maintain their relationship through the first two years of college and called it quits on amicable terms.

Throughout his collegiate career, he'd had countless internships and jobs, most of which came through INROADS, a program focused on increasing ethnic diversity in Fortune 500 companies. This is how Toussaint got his start in finance with his first job at Fleet Bank and was able to parlay that into two summer internships with Merrill Lynch. It was at Merrill Lynch during his senior year where he met

Tara, a student at Seton Hall University. She was attractive, smart, and caring, which is an essential characteristic for Toussaint, and should be for other young men.

Upon graduation from Rutgers with a degree in finance, Toussaint would move back home before he and Tara moved in together. While we were all very proud of his accomplishment of being the first in the Crew to graduate college, it was also the most trying time of our budding adult relationship. Our family, like many others, had established a tradition of having graduation celebrations. One night at a family dinner, Toussaint tells us that he doesn't want a party. Instead, he wanted us to do what Tara's family did for her graduation gift—create a T-shirt with his picture on it for support. This went against our family tradition, but it was also belittling to our collective efforts. All of us were stunned and angry at this outburst and disrespect. Imani was really upset and thought this warranted a physical altercation. There are times when parents are faced with tough decisions in the moment. How should I react to this issue? I did not want to fall into the trap of being influenced by his peers. Many of his friends were getting more significant gifts than a party. Despite the initial drama, Toussaint had a great graduation party. The importance of the tradition is that other folks were part of the village that should have the opportunity to celebrate this milestone.

Adding to his frustration, Toussaint had to sleep on the couch when he returned home from school as all of the bedrooms were full. The only bed available was a pullout sofa in the family room. In Toussaint's mind, the fact that he graduated from college and was gainfully employed meant that he should have the bedroom. He complained that while Sekou dropped out of college and still had a bedroom felt backward. In truth, I had planned to give Toussaint the room but decided to wait. I knew all too well how angry words can tear relationships apart that may take years to repair—if ever. It was clear to me then, while Toussaint and I had an open relationship, he needed his own room and space to grow into the man he was becoming.

His entrance into the financial services field set in motion a journey he is still on today. Personally, it is very significant because few African Americans work in this arena, and he was committed to having a career in the business. Toussaint and Tara were dating for four years at that point and shared a home. It seemed that marriage was on the horizon. I sensed, however, he wanted something more significant for himself. Despite just being three years removed from Rutgers, Toussaint turned his attention to a full-time MBA. The fact that he pursued this in the wake of the Global Financial Crisis in 2008 was not lost on anyone. While Toussaint and Tara traveled to Dartmouth, Michigan, and Virginia, it was clear to me that Toussaint desired to be in New York City, and work on Wall Street was going to win. Ultimately, he attended NYU Stern School of Business on a full-tuition scholarship and decided to go that route without Tara. We spent many hours talking through his decision, and I knew he wouldn't have gotten the experience he desired if he chose anywhere else to attend. As a proud Baba, Toussaint is the first of the Crew to complete undergraduate and graduate school. He was appointed to the emerging markets desk at Deutsche Bank and has worked at Goldman Sachs and Morgan Stanley in the years since. He has accomplished a very important goal, which certainly inspired all of us.

What has made me more proud, however, is Toussaint's growth to be a better brother, particularly his relationship with Sekou. I have always wanted them to be closer, but as a parent, it is important never to force these behaviors. It always seemed like there was some underlying jealousy; Toussaint was jealous of Sekou's athletic, musical, and academic talents early on; Sekou was jealous of Toussaint's financial stability later on. It took years for them to learn about each other at different speeds. When Sekou became a parent, I think their relationship reached a level that I always wanted. What was always evident to me, that they had more in common than they realized, finally dawned on them. Toussaint wasn't selfish. Sekou wasn't reclusive. They needed each other, and I am proud to say that it is a lesson that they both have learned and taken to heart.

*Toussaint toddler years.*

*Toussaint elementary years.*

*Soccer goals.*

*Brothers.*

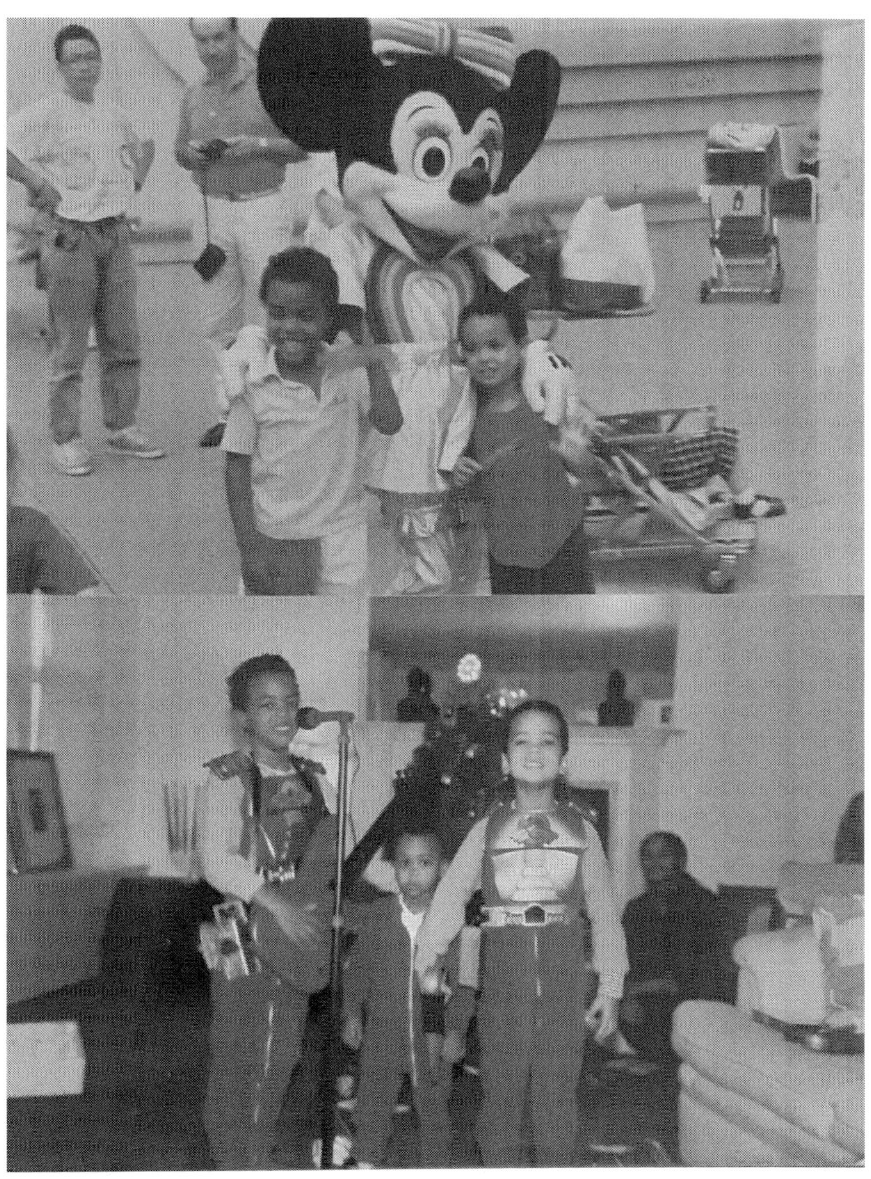

# CHAPTER 9

# IMANI

*"Yes, Mother. I can see that you are flawed. You have not hidden it. That is your greatest gift to me."*

**— Alice Walker**

Imani Nefertari Simone was born early on Sunday morning, February 22, 1987, at Beth Israel Hospital in Newark, New Jersey. Her flair for the dramatic started from her breech birth. Fortunately, the doctor was very talented and was able to accomplish a healthy delivery despite the danger. Imani's birth made all of us happy—especially her mother. After birthing two sons, having a daughter was a blessing. Marilyn and I often talked about how grateful she was to have a daughter. Girls bring kindness and loving behaviors to any family, which adds a special touch. Imani, meaning "faith," was named after the ideal and seventh principle of Kwanzaa. When your third child is born, it takes faith in her, our family, and community. Imani's middle names honor the Egyptian queen Nefertari and her aunt Simone.

Early on, Marilyn had aspirations for Imani to continue down her path of fashion and modeling. Imani was also a "pretty" baby with chubby cheeks and brownish-black curly hair. As they grew older, Imani and her siblings would debate who looked more like their mother. Imani especially wanted to look more like Marilyn, as it made her feel closer to her mother, despite Marilyn's absence. Being a middle child and the first daughter significantly shaped Imani's world view. From an early age, she advocated for justice. Her sense of fairness and equality would serve her well. At four years old, she was concerned about her mother's well-being and often wanted to make sure her mom was included in everything we did, both inside the house and outside. During the family separation, when we were looking for a new home while looking at the new house, Imani asked, "Where's mommy's room?" By that time, Marilyn and I had been living in separate bedrooms. Imani didn't realize the changes unfolding in our family. Out of all of the Crew, she was the most vocal about the absence of her mother.

Being in the house with two older brothers who liked to play rough, and later having a younger sister who had major health challenges at an early age, Imani flourished. She was very verbal at an early age and grew fast. Imani was determined to compete with her brothers, and whoever else showed up on the scene. She excelled in school in all facets; academically, artistically, and athletically. She maintained and expanded the family tradition of honoring the Robeson legacy. Imani learned to read early, which was a significant factor in her success in school and career. She was popular in school and several activities. In her younger years, she played soccer, and her athletic ability made her a team favorite. Also, Imani joined the Pop Warner cheerleaders' squad. Once again, she was embraced as one of the leaders of the team as a captain.

*"Have faith*
*You're a child of God*
*And you were put here to win*
*Have faith in yourself*
*In family and God*
*Imani..."*
**— Kwanzaa for Young People**

In middle school, Imani added a new direction to our scholar-athlete family creed and became the student council president. This was a formal confirmation of her leadership ability and the harbinger of many leadership roles and upholding justice. I recall she had a fight with a boy on the bus who was harassing her and other students. Word got out of Imani's beat-down skills, and not many of her peers bothered her after that. Although Imani excelled in middle school academically, she faced some challenges socially. Her interest in boys created tension between her and I as well as among her friends. Some of the members of the village commented that she was "boy crazy," and they were worried about how things would turn out in her future.

During her time in middle school, I came across notes between her and a boy she liked. The letters were very alarming to me because they included explicit sexual references. I didn't tell her what I read, but I contacted the boy's mother and explained what I'd found. She was unaware of what the children had discussed but evidently did speak to her son. Not surprisingly, word got back to Imani that I found the notes, and for some time, she stopped talking to me. I didn't want to force or demand verbal communication, so Imani and I only communicated through letters during this tense period.

This became an ideal way for us to communicate, give both of us time to reflect on previous letters, and carefully think about how we wanted to respond. This way of communicating also eliminated the potential for contentious or heated discussions that would have only exacerbated the tension between Imani and me.

At this time, I was also trying to find something to take her focus off boys, so I had Imani join a step team, which turned out to be a profound blessing. I was well aware of the things that go on in the home after school when there is little to no adult presence. I did not want teenage pregnancy, unwanted sexual advances, or anything along those lines to happen to my girls. Although Imani may have still been "boy crazy," her energy was redirected to the step team and the Nia Dance Ensemble, an African dance group created by a few members of the "village." The group name highlighted the fifth principle of Kwanzaa, "Nia," which means purpose.

To help my Crew and some of their peers enrich their understanding of African culture, the children would practice and perform at various community events. Sekou and Toussaint were in the drum section, and Imani was among the leaders for the dance section—the dance instructors looked to Imani to keep the dancers on track. Most of the dancers had a solo step, and Imani was selected for the high profiled "Goddess" step. Leadership was a gift that came naturally for Imani. She graduated consistently on the honor roll, and as President of the Student Council, she gave the speech at graduation that wowed the audience with her oratorical skills. These successes prepared her for high school, and teachers were requesting that she be in their classes.

## Ain't I A Woman

Imani's academic and extracurricular success continued in high school. She joined the "Super Chiefs," Piscataway High School's marching band. The practices were very intense, and the band had the reputation of discipline and excellence, having won state champion titles for many years. Imani played the alto sax but was asked by the band director to lead a new section of the band by switching to the French horn. In addition to the band, she also played basketball, was enrolled in honors classes and had a part-time job as a cashier in a local grocery store.

Imani and her friends also revived the "All Class," the high school chapter of her previous step team. At times, the pressure of all of these activities was overwhelming, but Imani managed. Her sense of justice continued to manifest in her advocacy in high school. She was elected as president of the student government three years straight. She was also selected by the school's leadership team to participate in the interview panel for Vice Principal candidates.

Imani is intelligent, talented, popular, and beautiful, which meant that boys would come knocking to ask her to the prom. I had some anxiety about sending my daughters to the prom. I realize that going to the prom is a highly desired rite of passage among teens, and Imani went three times. The first time was in her sophomore year. Imani was excited about shopping for her dress, getting her hair and makeup done, and finding accessories that would make her glamorous for the event. Part of the process also included finding someone to go with that would alleviate my anxiety. The stories about the after-prom activities, especially going to the Jersey Shore for the weekend, were very uncomfortable for me. Although most of these stories probably had a lot of yeast, they still made any father uneasy. In Imani's case, there was no attraction to her date; it was a case of mutual convenience as both needed a date. When Imani attended the prom in her junior year, she was invited by her boyfriend. To ensure things went as desired, I placed a time limit on after prom events, much to Imani's displeasure. Although my decision was not popular, it was necessary, and the events went off without much fanfare.

The senior prom took on a life all its own. The dress had to be extraordinary and very expensive. It also had to be as revealing as the school policy permitted. To accomplish this feat, it had to be taped in certain places. Imani wore a gold custom, handmade sequin gown with a deep neckline, high slit, and low cut-out back. The dress was even more special to Imani as it was designed at a boutique in Greenwich Village, New York. To take this prom to the next level, Imani's date was an athlete from another school. Of course, Imani was very sad about the time limits I required. She protested because Sekou and Toussaint were not given time restraints for their proms. She accused me of being sexist as the rules were different for her brothers. I was willing to accept that label as I knew the different expectations of gender at these events and did not want Imani to end up in an undesirable situation. Luckily, Imani was so pleased with how all of her prom preparations came together that she had a great time despite her initial protests.

Imani's senior prom will also stand out in her memory and the Crew's memory for less joyous reasons. Up until this time, I had been guarding the extent of their mother's bipolar disorder. They had never witnessed episodes as I had in the past. Marilyn was initially very involved in the prom preparation process: attending dress fittings, helping to pay for various expenses, and even securing a celebrity makeup artist who was an old friend from her modeling days. However, as the prom preparation continued, Marilyn's behavior became increasingly erratic. She began missing appointments, breaking promises, and seeming less stable. The Crew was unaware that Marilyn was on the cusp of a full-blown bipolar episode.

At one point, Marilyn, visibly intoxicated, showed up at our home with two men none of us knew. All of us were extremely uncomfortable, and for the Crew, this was the first time they had seen their mother behave this way. One of my goals was to make sure home was a safe space. There will be crazy things that happen in the world, but home should provide solace. I was furious and told those men not to ever make the mistake again of showing up and violating my home. Toussaint was also extremely sad and frustrated, asking, "Why does my mom have to do this?" The cloud over the senior prom became very significant. Imani later asked, "Can I get what mommy has?" I replied, "No, you will not get this."

Despite these challenges at the end of her senior year, Imani graduated from high school with a very impressive list of accomplishments, including student government president and a ranking of 16, landing her in the top 3% of her class academically. As the college decision-making process unfolded, a few of her peers gained acceptance into very prestigious colleges and universities, and Imani was hopeful for the same. My counsel to all of my children was to minimize student loan debt. If we had to incur educational debt, it would be for graduate school, not undergraduate.

Imani's best offer came from Rutgers, an annual $10,000 Carr scholarship. Imani cried when she realized that after all her accomplishments for so many years, she would attend a university around the corner from our home. Fortunately, Imani figured out how to make RU work for her. She studied abroad in South Africa, which was another first for our family. She continued her leadership and advocacy efforts as a board member in the Douglass Black Students Congress and held various corporate internships as a member of the INROADS Program.

All of these experiences prepared Imani for successful post-graduate pursuits. First, she was selected for a prestigious Johnson & Johnson Fellowship, which included a full-tuition scholarship to the Master of Communications Program at Rutgers. Again, Imani excelled in this program, graduating with a 4.0 G.P.A., participating in various conferences in the U.S. and abroad, and ultimately securing a job offer to create a corporate philanthropy program for a global IT firm. After a few years in the work world, Imani followed in Toussaint's footsteps and pursued her MBA on a full-tuition fellowship at the University of Michigan. At Michigan, Imani continued her leadership pursuits and was elected to various boards of student organizations. She took her global citizenship to a new level, visiting, studying, and working in dozens of countries that serve her well in her career today.

*True sistas.*

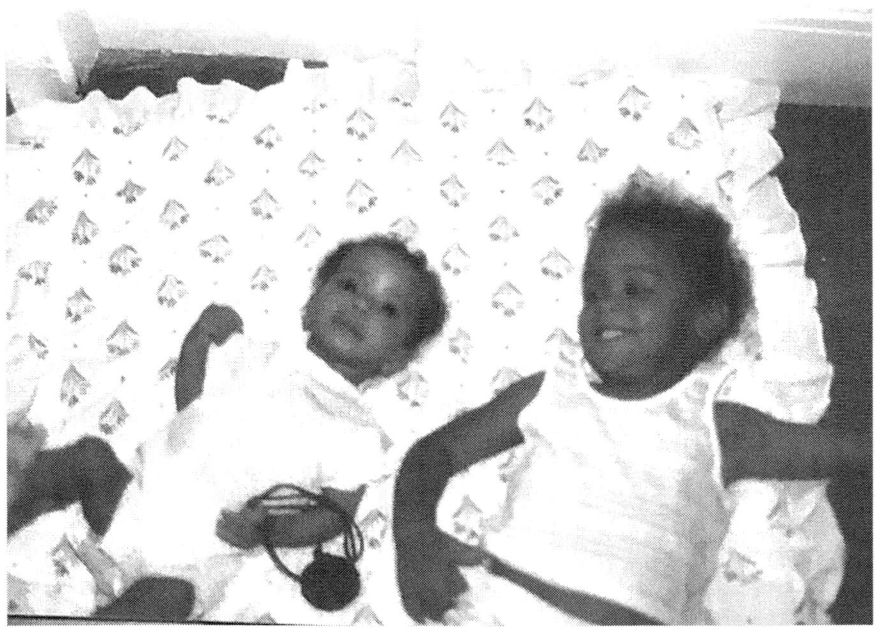

*Imani through the years.*

# CHAPTER 10

## NAEEMAH

*"Sisterhood is important because we are all we have to stand on. We have to stand near and by each other, pray for one another, and share the joys and the difficulties that women face in the world today."*

— **Ntozake Shange**

Naeemah Ife Safiya was born in the evening on Tuesday, January 24, 1989. Like her sister and brothers, Naeemah was a healthy and "pretty" baby. Her name means benevolence (grace), a loved one who is wise. Unknown at the time was how significant her name would become. During Marilyn's pregnancy, there were a few family challenges, mainly financial. With three children in school or childcare, the financial strain was very hard, especially since I was the only person working. The other major issue was the health of Naeemah's maternal grandmother, Loretta, who had breast cancer and didn't share the prognosis with the family that she only had six months to live. When Naeemah was about three months old, her maternal grandmother passed.

The pain this caused Marilyn was immense for two reasons. First, the shock and surprise of how gravely ill her mother was and given the fact that no one explained this clearly. Second, she felt guilty that she had not been able to help or spend much time before her mother passed.

Loretta decided for the benefit of her daughters and the family, not to disclose the severity of her illness as both daughters were pregnant. The courage to face cancer without sharing the news with your loved ones is an extraordinary act of courage and sacrifice—we are all grateful for Loretta's courage.

Loretta's death would play a significant factor in all of our lives sooner than we realized. A few months after her death, Naeemah was diagnosed with heart disease, which required major surgery. During a routine well visit, the doctor heard Naeemah struggling to breathe. She explained to Marilyn that Naeemah had to go to the emergency room ASAP. Marilyn took her to Children's Hospital in Newark. After a series of tests, the results showed that Naeemah had an artery that had to be transplanted from the right side to the left side of her heart. The ex-rays revealed her heart was almost twice the size it's supposed to be for her age, which resulted from several possible small heart attacks.

We were frightened and confused. After more research and discussions with Naeemah's doctors, we learned that it is a congenital disability that many people die from because it is often undiagnosed. And while Naeemah appeared healthy and seemed to develop more slowly than the rest of the Crew, her heart issue had delayed her growth. She would sweat much more, which was evidence that she was not getting enough oxygen in her blood.

The procedure was a success, and Naeemah stayed in the hospital for several weeks. Marilyn stayed with Naeemah to comfort her. The trauma of this moment was more significant than anything we had collectively faced. The rest of the 'crew' were too young to understand, and no one in either family had suffered a health issue on this scale. Seeing your child so close to death with tubes and medical equipment was the scariest situation I had ever faced. Before Loretta's death, no one had ever died or been gravely ill in our family. We were blessed with a very competent medical staff. There were many medical visits for years to make sure her heart was functioning correctly. Thankfully, Naeemah has not had any other significant health challenges.

*"...that I'll be loving you always*
*Until the rainbow burns the stars out in the sky (always)*
*Until the ocean covers every mountain high (always)*
*Until the dolphin flies and parrots live at sea (always)*
*Until we dream of life and life becomes a dream..."*
***— Stevie Wonder***

The Creator and universe will prepare us, although we usually don't realize it during the moment. My mother and father would eventually have significant medical challenges, and Naeemah's medical situation helped prepare me for these later life's trials. Due to Naeemah's early diagnosis, the Crew has often stated that Naeemah is my favorite child. I have explained many times that my personality as a person and father is to be protective, and given all of the stress and toll of her medical crisis, the bond formed between us is hard to change.

## Coming Up the Rear

As Naeemah grew, she had to find her place amongst her siblings. Sekou and Toussaint still played rough, and Imani was still trying to keep up. Not long after Naeemah turned three years old, our family dynamic changed. Marilyn and I separated, and the children and I moved together to Piscataway. While I explained that we were moving and mommy would not be there, the significance of this could not be fully understood at their young ages.

Naeemah and Imani were hoping to follow in their mother's footsteps of being models or working in the fashion industry. At an early age, they played dress up and wanted to do "girly" activities like having tea parties and fashion shows. As Naeemah got older, she developed a strong interest in being a makeup artist. I was not useful in this area. Fortunately, some of the members of the village stepped up and assisted. This support would prove to be a crucial factor in raising my daughters, and it's a theme that came up repeatedly on our journey.

The move to Piscataway was related to my change in employment. I took a Director position at Middlesex County College, and both Imani and Naeemah were in the daycare together on the campus for a short time. From the beginning, Naeemah was creative and loved arts and crafts. Her first-grade teacher, Mrs. Hanley, gave her a bookbag full of Crayola products, and Naeemah could not contain herself! Naeemah was able to form positive relationships with her teachers and become a favorite to many of them. She was timid as a child, but once she got comfortable with you, her personality would shine. One of the things that Naeemah loved was for me to come to her class for *any* reason. She was a daddy's girl to the core.

When she was young, Naeemah formed a vital friendship that would last to this day. She will tell you the story of her and Seyelle on the playground in kindergarten, and Seyelle walked up to her and said, "Hi, I'm Seyelle. Do you wanna be friends?" And the rest is history. By way of Seyelle, Naeemah adopted the whole Collier family and eventually decided that they were her god-family. The Colliers have been with us on our family journey for years.

Naeemah followed Imani's lead in many cases and did well in school for the most part. She was popular amongst her diverse group of peers. Like Imani, she was also elected President of the Student Council and gave the commencement address in middle school. I remember her all-white outfit was a significant aspect of this momentous occasion. As there were many highs for Naeemah during this time, it proved to be a tough few years for her. In seventh grade, almost all of her friends stopped talking to her for months. She was so hurt. Thankfully, Seyelle stuck by her. I'm sure if I asked her what the issue was, no one would remember. But this incident had a lasting effect on her. Fortunately, there were a few talented and committed staff who helped Naeemah and her peers work through those issues. She also followed the family tradition of being in the band and played percussion in middle school, including an African drum solo at a holiday concert. Naeemah's favorite middle school highlight would be the talent and fashion show she and her friends participated in their eighth-grade year. The group of girls practiced at all of our homes for weeks. They even went to New York City to find their outfits. The show was a big hit, and we still watch the performance for laughs.

High school for Naeemah was a time of many changes. Imani was a junior, so most of the faculty already knew the Davis family. This was a double-edged sword for her because her siblings had created high expectations. At the same time, she had a pretty good safety net with the network her siblings, especially the one Imani had created. After auditioning at the end of her freshman year, Naeemah was selected as the drum major for Piscataway High School. This was the first time the school had an African American in this role, and she was also the youngest drum major. She enjoyed her high profile status and was cognizant of the fact she was the last of the Davis clan to leave her mark on the school. Many teachers and staff were helpful and preferred that she was in their class. Math was a subject that she struggled with, like Toussaint, but she was able to pass with the help of tutors. Ironically, Naeemah was chosen to be a part of the group that prepared young girls and women to study STEM, and she was featured in a few local news articles.

As much as Naeemah flourished academically and socially, our relationship became very strained when she chose not to respect the rules of our home. This behavior started freshman year and continued throughout high school. As a parent, I recognized that this was a way of acting out to get the attention of her siblings—even if it meant putting negative attention on herself. During this time, the village was crucial. Mrs. Collier, Naeemah's godmother, helped out on many occasions when I was at my wit's end on how to get my youngest daughter to follow directions.

Like Imani, Naeemah attended several proms. As I wouldn't allow my children to go to any proms as a freshman, the first one she attended was her sophomore year. She and Imani, a senior at the time, went to the prom together, and they loved it! For her junior prom, she went with a popular guy on the basketball team. Naeemah always says this was the most fun prom for her. For her senior prom, she insisted on a dress that had to be custom made as I had allowed Imani to do it previously. We went to New York City to find the perfect fabric, similar to what Imani had done. The satin, champagne-colored dress was V-cut with crystals sewn all over. There were revealing parts of this dress that I did not like, but Naeemah was happy, and she looked beautiful. She attended the senior prom with a young man from another school, and she also attended his senior prom. Despite both her and Imani's protest to extend the prom curfew, my time limits remained in effect.

As far as college was concerned, Naeemah was determined to attend an HBCU, preferably in Atlanta. She was part of The New Horizons program designed to assist high school students in attending college. The program was based in Plainfield, but open to students from other communities. A few of Naeemah and Imani's friends attended. A vital aspect of the program was to conduct a college tour, including some of the well-known schools like Spelman and Morehouse. This trip was a significant influence on Naeemah's desire to attend college in the "ATL." We agreed that attending an HBCU would be great, but financially it wasn't possible. Spelman was her first choice, and Clarke Atlanta came in right behind. Naeemah, like her siblings, attended Rutgers somewhat kicking and screaming.

Thankfully, Rutgers turned out to be the right move for her. She was close enough to home when she needed support and far enough to operate independently. It was of utmost importance for Naeemah to get out from under my rules. This was a necessary distance for us, and it helped strengthen our relationship. She lived on campus. Once, she walked home because she had a severe cold and knew that I had a natural remedy of garlic, orange juice, zinc, goldenseal, echinacea, and oil of oregano. Once she understood the sacrifices I had made for her and all of her siblings, she gained another level of respect for me.

In Naeemah's junior year at RU, she decided to study abroad in South Korea. Imani had previously studied abroad in South Africa. This was a real accomplishment for Naeemah, as she had never traveled internationally and definitely not alone. As the youngest, we all cared for Naeemah, and she had the most support for a long time. This trip was a chance for her to be independent, and she stepped up for the challenge. When she returned, it was clear that she was "over" RU and ready to take the next steps to broaden her senior year's horizons. She started working for a few of Rutgers' opportunity programs, somewhat following my path as an academic advisor. We both worked for programs that had the goal of helping underrepresented demographics reach higher education.

Since then, Naeemah's first job after graduating from Rutgers has taken many turns. It is an uncomfortable and emotional moment as a parent to watch children become who they are. Naeemah always wanted to become a chef since she was a child, but as with all of the Crew, a college education was a primary requirement. Naeemah now owns a bakery business where she has the freedom to express her art through edible creations. Running a small business is not fun and games, and as a family, we've seen Naeemah deal with the ups and downs that go with the territory. The support system that we have built over time comes in handy when each of us needs more support than the other. Her business name, Sweet Dreams Boutique Bakery, comes from the nickname my mother gave her when she was a baby and one that we still call her to this day—Dream.

*Naeemah...probably thinking, why are they looking at me?*

*Miracle child. A dream fulfilled.*

*Naeemah through the years.*

*Three cheers for the Davis sisters!*

*Naeemah the dancer.*

# CHAPTER 11

# Flying Solo

*"A life is not important except in the impact it has on other lives."*
***— Jackie Robinson***

To say that 1989 was a traumatic year for the Davis family is an understatement. A few years prior, the position in New Brunswick was defunded by the state, and I was transferred to RU Newark. The director, James Ramsey, appointed me as an EOF counselor. My duties were to provide academic, financial aid, and personal counseling to minority students. I immensely enjoyed this role; forming a bond with the students and assisting them through the challenges they faced was very rewarding. It was also the first time I conducted group counseling sessions, which helped prepare me to teach. I also had a part-time appointment to conduct group counseling sessions with high school students on Saturdays in a pre-college program. This experience was extremely beneficial when I started my pre-college program for high school students in Piscataway.

My boss, Mr. Ramsey, was promoted to a higher administrative position, and his replacement felt somewhat threatened by a few of the staff, including me. I was appointed as the assistant director of the Office for African American Student Services at NYU. This new position was a significant step in my professional career. It was the first time I was not working at RU or in the EOF program. It was also my first time serving as an administrator. NYU needed to improve the retention and success of African American students. To accomplish these goals, the office was tasked with developing mentor, tutorial, and related student services to ensure African American student success. The office was newly created, and I was the first person to serve in the role. Fortunately, the administrative structure at NYU was similar to RU. I was comfortable with my role and what the director and I were accomplishing. This change did make Marilyn uncomfortable. She was nervous about me being back in NYC. My commute was also extremely long, and sometimes my Crew would ask if I would be home before they went to sleep. If I missed the train, I had to wait an hour before the next one.

Sadly, a few months after my appointment, my mother-in-law, Loretta, passed. The impact of this tragedy on our family was immense. As I mentioned, Loretta was diagnosed with breast cancer and given six months to live. After Loretta's death, my children and I lost Marilyn physically and emotionally. Marilyn took her mother's death very hard because it was sudden, and there was a sense of guilt for not being in Milwaukee during that time. Clearly, I was unable to stay as focused as needed on my duties at work. Within a short time, I left NYU. I wanted to move my family to North Carolina, where my mother lived. I visited multiple times, but the Creator had a better plan. I was appointed as director of the Middlesex County College (MCC) New Brunswick Center, a small branch campus. My duties were to coordinate various academic courses and social service programs. The main campus also had on-site childcare, which worked out well for my daughters and me.

Prior to that year, Marilyn had been suffering from bipolar episodes more frequently. I took her to several doctors, and they prescribed medication. For over a year, the medication was not helping and appeared to make matters worse. My father came to live with me for a short time to help out with the Crew. Marilyn's family came to New Jersey and took her back to Milwaukee in 1990. After several months, my sisters and others were on my case telling me that the children needed their mother and that I should have Marilyn come back home right away. I listened to my family, and Marilyn came back to spend the holidays with the Crew.

In January 1991, I was celebrating my birthday. Marilyn had another episode and was paranoid. She paced the floor and scratched her fingers until they bled. It was extremely intense to observe. Those at the party were in shock and had no idea what I was going through. It was clear that we made the right decision to keep her away from the children. After that incident, I moved into the spare bedroom, praying each day to figure out what to do. I remained in my own room the entire year. It was clear that the marriage was done but was ambivalent about taking care of my Crew.

I talked to a friend who was a nurse about getting Marilyn appropriate care. I had such mixed emotions about taking her to a psychiatric ward as I had heard so many horror stories. I decided to take her to the hospital because my friend said that I needed to take her or else I would be responsible if she harmed herself. I then talked to my sister Jean, and she made it clear that I had to tell Marilyn's family. I was surprised that Marilyn's family were aware of her bipolar episodes. Yet, they were also unsure of the best mental health environment for proper care. Marilyn went back to Milwaukee and stayed with her family.

After the first year of settling into a routine in Piscataway, Marilyn's family called to see if I would send the children to Milwaukee in the summer to visit their mother. It was an extremely tough decision, and I told them I would let them know in a few days. My emotions were in high gear. The Crew were ages 3, 5, 7, and 9. I started thinking about my incident with Deidre, and her husband barring me from seeing or contacting my daughter Monifah. I realized that I never wanted my children to say that I kept them from their mother if she wanted to see them. I sent them to Milwaukee for a week. I am grateful that Marilyn did what was best for the children and sent them back to New Jersey. I know that I am lucky that she trusted I would raise them in a healthy way.

## A Broader Impact

Within a few months, my employer, MCC, expanded the facilities and added new programs that lead to the construction of a new site. Given my prior experiences in New Brunswick, I was able to leverage my connections to benefit my current position. I also added a community Kwanzaa celebration, which was a huge success. I met LeDerick Horne, a poet, and tutor who I adopted as my younger brother. He was a crowd favorite as his "poetic acrobatics" inspired many.

During my tenure at MCC, I created the Epic Vision Pre College Program for Piscataway High School students. It was modeled after the RU Newark effort. LeDerick served as a math tutor, Tomeka Thompson was a science tutor, and there were a few other folks who helped with this effort. The goal was to ensure that students received adequate support in their academic pursuits. I chose tutors of color who were competent and deviated from the stereotype that people of color were not good in math and science. Society fails to recognize that children of color in suburban communities face similar issues to children in urban communities; only the scale is different.

Despite my success at MCC for 12 years, I was not reappointed to my position due primarily to political reasons. The Creator had another plan in place, which resulted in my appointment as a trainer in Positive Behavior Support, an intervention designed to improve school climate and reduce suspensions and the number of children placed in special education. I trained school staff across New Jersey, which afforded me a state-wide role as opposed to a limited local responsibility.

## Flying Low

I recall back to school night, and the Crew was excited about me meeting their teachers. Some of the teachers have used incentives to encourage parents to attend. The class with the most parental participation will win a prize, a pizza party, or cookies. The pressure was on to be present.

I clearly understand and value the importance of school and home communication efforts. Given the unique circumstances of our family dynamic, I intended to be there for each child every step of the way. At that time, the Crew was in four different schools! So I worked on a plan to "fly low" to make all four meetings. I arrived early to explain to the teacher my situation in hopes that each one understood my request and suggested an alternative time to meet.

In a situation where my child had challenges, then I was prepared to stay longer. Fortunately, since this happened early in the school year, there were not many issues. In most cases, the teachers were pleased and, at times, surprised to see only me and that I wanted my child to excel academically and to participate in extracurricular activities. Over time, as I became more familiar with the school staff, and they learned more about our family, the parent-teacher process was not as challenging.

Yet my daily duties were just as intense as trying to juggle four schools. Our daily process was to get up and have breakfast together. While the Crew ate breakfast, I'd start dinner, as lunch was already made. They'd go to school by bus, or I'd drop them off at the before school program. The next stop was for me to get work and then rush to get them from the after school program. We would usually have an activity or practice to go to, which meant a quick stop home, and then out again. Based on whether all or just some of the Crew participating in the activity determined the next step. Also, I had to make these efforts in addition to deciding how long I could stay at the event as I may have had to go grocery shopping or do laundry. Sometimes I was fortunate that another member of the village would either pick up or drop off the Crew after an activity.

All of the meals were fairly consistent and some more popular than others, lol. Our family was mainly vegetarian, so I would usually plan dinner around a starch like rice, potatoes, or pasta. Spinach pie with potatoes would get mixed reviews based on whether I added cheese or less mustard. Their favorites were Sunday breakfast. I followed my father's tradition of home fries, waffles, or pancakes, with an omelet. No matter what I cooked, my sons were always still hungry. I nicknamed them big and little Jurassic.

# CHAPTER 12

# TROUBLE AHEAD

*"Character is power."*
***— Booker T. Washington***

I believe all parents desire the same thing for their children: to stay out of trouble, do well in school, and achieve greater things than we ever imagined. While I have no fool-proof parenting 101 advice, I can say that much of my decision-making was based on my upbringing. I desired to ensure that a large part of their identity consisted of values and principles. Above all else, I wanted my Crew, to be honest, moral human beings, and to be active, positive forces in their communities. I valued my role as Baba and did my best to steer them in the right direction, but at the end of the day, there are hereditary factors and lessons that they can only learn from their own experiences. Each of them faced difficult times during adolescence and teenage years, which ultimately made them stronger.

## The 11th Commandment: Thou Shall Not Get Caught

As a child, I remember my uncle teasing me about "trying to find money." He laughed so hard when I searched the sofa cushions, drawers, and even in the kitchen. I can still hear his voice and hearty laugh. I thought no one saw me steal two dollars off the kitchen table. I imagine my parents felt the same stress that I did as each of my Crew had their own "finding money" adventures.

Sekou was definitely the worst. He would lie while we as a family saw him steal. His sibling's money would often turn up missing, and he would somehow "magically" know the amount they lost. One particular episode was during a visit to my mothers' house when he stole five dollars from his cousin. When mom called to tell me, she asked me not to give him a beating, but to take something he valued to help him learn the lesson. It seemed to work for a short time. Despite beatings and punishment, Sekou's stealing continued for many years. Finding creative and effective solutions for my children's misbehavior was a continuous challenge.

Toussaint observed his brothers' behavior and punishment and chose to avoid it most of the time. He hung out with friends who stole cookies and other items from the school cafeteria or other places. There were a few cases of Toussaint also "finding" his younger sister's money. I believe Toussaint was with Sekou when he and a few friends stole a Wu-Tang Clan CD from Walmart.

Imani also had "stolen moments" stealing lip gloss and other toiletries. She also had a few capers involving her car. I insisted that the Crew not let their friends drive their vehicles. Imani decided not to heed my message and loaned her car to a friend who had very risky behavior. The friend then let Naeemah, who didn't have a license drive. Fortunately, the Creator protected the children around the corner, where Naeemah crashed into the neighbor's yard.

On Super Bowl Sunday, Kohl's called to tell me Naeemah was caught shoplifting and would be released when I came to the store. She had stolen lip gloss, eyeliner, and mascara. The embarrassment and potential punishment were not enough to dissuade her behavior. Over time, I think she continued this act but was guided by the $11^{th}$

Commandment: thou shall not get caught. I had a similar moment when I was caught stealing a jacket from Macy's. I was terrified of the beating I knew was coming. Despite a terrible beating, I also continued to steal. Peer pressure was undoubtedly a factor. My friends and I would have contests of who could steal the most. The saying, "The sins of the father are passed on to their children," has some validity.

The macro aspect of these behaviors perpetuates negative stereotypes of African Americans and contributes to mass incarceration. Fortunately, everyone outgrew the stealing phase, and there were no criminal charges or the involvement of law enforcement.

## Letting Go

I have found that the hardest part of parenting is allowing my adult children to make their own decisions. I never thought this would be an issue for me, but frankly, it has become one. I instinctively want to make things easier for my Crew and not let them take the long road to what I believe the ultimate solution should have been. I find myself pressing each one about their employment, life choices, or dating. To their credit, they push back and remind me that they are grown, but will come to me for my input when needed.

These past few years, Sekou has required more attention than the rest. He has struggled with the music business for several years. When Sekou and his girlfriend came to tell me that she was pregnant, I insisted that if it was a girl that her name is Nia, because Sekou needed "purpose" in his life. I'm clear that my perspective is outside of the norm, but I'm also really clear of the value and significance of African names. If it had been a boy, his name would have been "Samori," which means African king, and his middle name would have been "Mandela."

There was a lot of tension between Sekou and me during that time. I got up and went to work every day, and he was still lying in bed at home. I gave him a window of six months to find a path to support himself. He enrolled in Rutgers and graduated with a degree in Communications. It was a blessing that turned out to produce phenomenal results.

On January 1, 2014, we welcomed Sekou's daughter, Nia, into the family. At that time, Sekou had three DUI's and was spared jail time in each instance. His license was suspended, he paid hefty fines, and performed community service. However, the fourth time, the judge ordered him to serve six months in jail on Valentine's Day, 2014. Naeemah was with me in court. She cried as they took her brother away in handcuffs. Sekou did the opposite of everything I taught him. As a family, we have been health-conscious, so drinking and driving are out of the question. I taught my Crew to minimize the window for the police to stop you, and more importantly, do not give them an obvious reason to harass you.

It was incredibly painful to see my son in that situation, but he put himself there. No parent wants to see their child incarcerated. I was angry, disappointed, and hurt. Jail time was a lesson that he had to learn. I know I'm not the only parent who told their kids, "I'm not coming to see you in jail. There should be no reason for your a _ _ to be in jail!" Sekou made me eat my words. I visited him every weekend and encouraged him with empowering words and books to read. We had fruitful discussions on changing his life. I even took Nia to see him on occasion.

**Black Fact:** New Jersey has a Black/white incarceration ratio of 12:1. In other words, a Black adult is 12 times more likely than a white adult to be incarcerated in New Jersey.[1]

The United States criminal justice system is the largest in the world.[2] At year-end 2015, over 6.7 million individuals:

1) were under some form of correctional control in the United States, including 2.2 million incarcerated in federal, state, or local prisons and jails.
2) The U.S. is a world leader in its rate of incarceration, dwarfing nearly every other nation.
3) Such broad statistics mask the racial disparity that pervades the U.S. criminal justice system and African Americans. African Americans are more likely than white Americans to be arrested; once arrested, they are more likely to be convicted; and once convicted, and they are more likely to experience lengthy prison sentences. African-American adults are 5.9 times more likely to be incarcerated than whites, and Hispanics are likely to be 3.1 times. See also, The Color of Justice: Racial and Ethnic Disparity in State Prisons by the Sentencing Project.[3]
4) Racial and ethnic disparities among women are less substantial than among men but remain prevalent.

Whenever I am asked to give an opening message at a Black history or other events to discuss our people, I start with graphs of the State of New Jersey. Despite being a wealthy and diverse blue state, we lead the country in disproportionate incarceration numbers. Over 20 years ago, I was on a youth service commission to look at juveniles in the prison system. Twenty years later, we are in the same place. Even though the number of people who are incarcerated has declined, we are still overrepresented. Keeping in mind that Chris Christie was the only Republican Governor in New Jersey for several years. Why has not much changed in our communities since the 60s? Part of it is because of the narrative that we chose to follow. Until we change our narrative, we will not be able to accomplish the great things that we are capable of doing.

Visiting jail facilities in New York and New Jersey were not new to me. Seeing Sekou in jail impacted me because my father was incarcerated three times. The difference is that when I visited daddy or others, I was able to interact and socialize with them. Visiting Sekou took place behind a glass. Sekou being locked up was hard on the Crew—they were traumatized. Our only consolation was that the Creator blessed us with a family friend who was a Corrections Officer, and he watched over Sekou in the less dangerous part of the prison. I recall when my father was locked up, he had to make weapons for his safety. When Sekou came home, we had a family welcome home celebration as we were all relieved that he was out and had a great opportunity to be a father and start over. We are all proud that Sekou is becoming the man he was destined to be. My daddy used to say there is an easy way to learn and a hard way to learn. Sekou had to learn the hard way.

*Sekou and my granddaughter, Nia, 2019.*

## Dating Chronicles

I was absolutely tough on my daughters as it relates to dating. I did not allow them to get serious with boys while they were in high school. I held my ground and was stricter on the girls because there was more at stake. I wanted them to graduate college, become professionals, and go to the next step in their romantic relationships. Yes, I was harder on my daughters than my sons, and I had a good reason. There was a remote possibility of Imani or Naeemah bringing a child home, and I wanted to be clear that I am not raising your children! I refused to normalize it for either my daughters or my sons. It was important for them to be prepared emotionally and financially before starting a family.

I remember we were at a high school basketball game, and a guy wanted to date Imani. He came up to me and introduced himself. Imani had a penchant for wanting to be with the cool guys. This guy certainly had a knucklehead reputation, so I was not going to endorse that.

When Imani was in college, I met this one guy, and I said, "What are your intentions with Imani? He replied, "Oh, I think Imani is dope!" Everybody in earshot knew he was in trouble. In reality, I thought he was a nice kid, but he was not prepared to have a real conversation. They dated, and it did not last too long. They tried to date a second time, and it did not work. I wanted my daughters and the knuckleheads to know that I was always paying attention. I told them both, "If you really want me to endorse the idea of your dating choice, it must be someone worthy of me meeting." In graduate school, Imani dated a white guy. Naeemah had met the guy previously and told me the day before I met him, "I don't think this guy is going to go very far." Naeemah was right.

I would prefer that my children date or marry an African American partner, but I have been more accepting of people for who they are.

The challenge I see is when people define themselves by their partner, which I believe becomes problematic. It's as if some of who they are is determined by the fact that the person they are dating is white. I will evaluate how I feel about the person someone in the Crew is dating based on how that person interacts with my child. I am more flexible about it now than I was before. I am comfortable with interracial dating with sincere people. When you think about it, the abolitionists sincerely wanted to end slavery and were just as committed to it as Blacks. If anything, the main question as a parent is that you have to pay attention to different stages of life. Whether it's taking their first steps, crossing the street, friends, driving, and dating, all of these stages require a different level of attention. As parents, we have to let our children know that we are on top of it.

Meanwhile, Toussaint was single, yet still friends with Tara, his girlfriend from college whom he lived with after graduation. He moved to New York to attend graduate school at NYU. Everyone thought he and Tara would get married. One of his roommates and friends from high school was now dating Tara without Toussaint's knowledge. Another friend shared this information with me. Toussaint was studying for a securities license exam when I received the news. Given the importance of the exam, I waited a few months before sharing what I was told. The pain in Toussaint's face will always stay with me. Helping my Crew through emotional challenges is a phenomenal task that I don't take lightly. Toussaint was betrayed by one of his high school friends for many years and girlfriend of several years. The healing process was long and painful. It took many years for him to be happy and be able to trust again.

# CHAPTER 13

# RIPPLES IN THE POND

*"Whoever controls the mind of our children controls the future."*
**— Julius Nyerere**

I have always wanted to teach at the college level. I had worked in an administrative capacity at three colleges over 30 years at Rutgers, NYU, and Middlesex County College. Throughout those years, I connected with students on a meaningful level, teaching them the skills needed to succeed in college. Specifically, time management, study techniques, tutoring, and mentoring. It was fulfilling to engage with students in that capacity as they were learning something and sharing their goals and achievements with me over the years. I am incredibly proud of my students and their accomplishments. Many of them send me emails to check-in and update me on their goals.

A few months after my mother passed, Naeemah and I were having lunch at an Ethiopian restaurant in our area. I ran into Gayle Tate, who I had known for years, and we made small talk. Gayle asked me in August if I wanted to teach at Rutgers in September. I was not emotionally ready at that time, but I told her that January would be better. Since I was one of the early graduates of the Rutgers African American Studies programs, which started in 1969.

I was among the first group of students to graduate in 1976. Also, I had gone to Egypt with Dr. Ben. More importantly, I had done a lot of independent learning on my own. Before that, I spoke all around the state and nationally on African American issues. When I received the syllabus, I made modifications to include financial literacy, the black aesthetic, art forms, and the media. I wanted to teach, and I had not formally applied. The universe had opened the path, and I was excited to take it as far as it leads me.

Teaching has and continues to be a profound blessing. I feel grateful for the opportunity. The ripples in the pond all of us make are sometimes not fully realized until later, but to honor our talents and legacy, we should do our best. I have received letters, emails, and words of praise from my former students because there was always a profound connection.

*Professor Davis,*

*I just wanted to say hello, and I hope your summer is going well! I hope this reaches you. Your class definitely inspired me to go a few directions, and I just wanted to share some of that with you!*

*I'm interning at the Truman National Security Project this summer, and it's been very eye-opening. Luckily, this organization puts a huge emphasis on diversity and inclusion because those practices produce the best outcomes. I am currently studying for my GRE as I want to work towards an International Relations Master's emphasizing on policy/ national security/peacekeeping.*

*In March, I was elected as the President of the Scarlet Chapter of the NAACP. I know that you're involved with the New Brunswick Chapter because Prof Bonadie does a great job of blasting everyone on social media! I talked with him and Bruce a lot because I want our chapters to work more closely. We're stronger when we're together, in my opinion.*

*I'm looking forward to that involvement, and if you have any advice/ guidance, I would love to talk sometime.*

*I really wanted to check in because I appreciated you and your class. That semester was pivotal in my life as I shifted what I was aiming for overall in life. I really look forward to hearing from you and hope you've been well!*

*L.B.*

*Professor Davis,*

*I was never fortunate enough to be in an African studies class. Whatever I had learned about African American history and culture was extremely limited in my history classes growing up. So coming into this class, almost everything that has been taught has been extremely valuable to me. Not only were the history lessons great, but the life lessons that were offered to us and the push we received to go out in the world, take the initiative, and make a change not only for ourselves but also for our fellow community members were inspiring.*

*Throughout the semester, I was able to make a ton of friends within the class. I had multiple chances to collaborate with classmates, which I found extremely fun and valuable to my learning and overall experience. Overall, this class has certainly been a highlight of the semester, even after switching to online remote instruction (although nothing beats being in class). I got to take a deep look into African American history and culture from a multitude of different perspectives. There are only a few memorable classes that I would say every college student walks out of changing the way they think about the world around them and leaving them with many new values, lessons, and perspectives. This class was certainly one of them for me.*

*The most valuable experience in this class was being able to share and have a space where myself, as a black woman, could speak freely without judgment or ridicule. I was able to learn about culture and history that I didn't even know existed. I was forced to go outside of my comfort zone and go into the unknown. Hearing about Steve Biko and cognitive dissonance and Paul Robeson and being a citizen of the world, and treating ourselves as worthy of such. It is true that when you know where you came from, you can know where you are going to. It will be easier to realize worth after seeing all the fighting and revolts and momentous events that took place to bring us to this place, 2020: where schools are integrated and black teachers are represented in higher numbers. We have a long way to go, but our progress is not to be ignored. I thank you, Professor, for creating this space for young minds like myself, and I wish to carry on the legacy of my ancestors and be a change agent for the better.*
*S.T.*

*Professor Davis,*
*Thank you so much for everything over the past couple of semesters I've had with you. You made me see things in a new perspective and encouraged me to go out and help others. You made me see the importance of being active in my community and engaging more with nationwide problems.*
*K.A.*

*Professor Davis,*

*I like that you not only discuss past events but how it affects us economically and socially today. The specifics of slavery were very interesting because they opened my eyes to how much worse I was taught in high school. I think it's important to have explicit and specific details about what happened in history to truly understand its effects throughout time.*

*You were always passionate about the course, which is encouraging. It's nice to see that you care about current topics and how we can change the community. I also appreciate how you make small comments when our assignments are graded, such as, "Good effort, thank you..." because it shows that you know how hard we work on the class.*

*J.C.*

*Professor Davis,*

*I like the "fire" you bring to the class, and I feel like your passion motivated me to listen closer and participate more in this class, even if I wasn't sure of the answer. I like how you encouraged participation to the point that I found myself speaking more in other classes as well.*

*N.R.*

*Professor Davis,*

*You have encouraged me to increase my financial literacy and also helped to educate me about my community. I went to a protest, and I cried for Eric Garner because, at that point, it became real to me. I was so emotional that I had to call my parents because I was confused, sad, and enraged all at the same time. I believe this class has given me a strong idea*

*of how I can fight to make the world a better place. I learned that we all have a role to play in this life, and it is up to us to play it well.*
*L. W.*

*Professor Davis,*

*Thank you for being very passionate about what you teach. It was easy to understand how you relayed the message so clearly, as well as the feelings behind them which enhanced my understanding. Your class is the reason Africana Studies is now my major and not just my minor. Thank you for sharing your passion and inspiring your students.*
*M.B.*

**Black Fact:** NJ Education System - The "achievement gap" has long been an issue facing educators in New Jersey and elsewhere. In 2020, the state released results of tests taken last spring, showing as much as a 38.4-point difference in the passing rate in third-grade language arts, between African-American and Asian students.

On that test, about 60 percent of black or African-American third-graders failed to achieve proficient scores, compared to 21.4 percent for Asian students and 31 percent for whites.

A student's economic circumstances matter, too. On the same third-grade test, only 40.2 percent of economically disadvantaged children were considered proficient, compared to 70.5 percent of their more well-off classmates.

Regarding school discipline in New Jersey, Black students were 5.4 times more likely to face out-of-school suspension than white students. In contrast, Hispanic students were 2.4 times more likely, according to a ProPublica analysis of 2015-16 federal data, which is worse than the national picture.

In addition, reports demonstrate that New Jersey and several other states have moved another substantial step toward a segregated future with no racial majority but severe racial stratification and division. Gary Orfield of the Los Angeles Times provides insight into how segregation has soared in American schools, and the government has largely ignored the problem.[4]

## *Reflections: My Trip to the Motherland*

In the Spirit of Lerato

July 18th, 2012

§ I arrive at Oliver Tambo Airport listening to Happy Birthday Madiba being sung by a choir.

The universe has blessed me to arrive on Mandela's birthday. The desire to visit South Africa has been high on my things-to-do list for many years. Nelson Mandela has been an inspiration for many people working for justice – the heroic struggle by the people of South Africa has given many people around the world hope. Working to end apartheid with its racist and brutal policies was a major victory – that nowhere in the world would we; people of the world interested in justice tolerate any form of racism.

Historical footnote: Oliver Tambo played a profound role in ending apartheid. He was among the founding members of the ANC Youth League (ANC YL) in 1944 and became its first National Secretary. He was elected President of the Transvaal ANCYL in 1948 and national vice-president in 1949. In the ANCYL, Tambo teamed up with Walter Sisulu, Nelson Mandela, Ashby Mda, Anton Lembede, Dr. William Nkomo, Dr. C.M.Majombozi and others to bring a bold, new spirit of militancy into the post-war ANC. Tambo left teaching soon after adopting the Program of Action and set up a legal partnership with

Nelson Mandela, the 1st African firm in the country. The firm soon became known as a champion of the poor, victims of apartheid laws with little or no money to pay their legal costs.

Having the opportunity to meet folks who were involved in the liberation efforts has been a true blessing. This journey is also a continuation of our African American long struggle for justice; Frederick Douglass, Marcus Garvey, Malcolm, King, among others all traveled and worked in the international arena. Working with the Global Literacy Project (GLP) to visit schools is an integral part of the trip.

Comrade Raks was involved in the struggle at 15 and arrested at age 19 imprisoned on Robben Island until he was 25; he was active in the ANC youth efforts to end apartheid. Since being released he has been instrumental in informing and highlighting literary contributions of South African writers and the broader arts and culture sector. His wife, Sindiswa, has also played an essential role in this effort. I had the chance to appreciate some of their work by attending two book club meetings, one with adults and others with children. Both had great readers and authors or, in the case of the children, a report on a book on the life of Stephen Biko. The adult meeting featured a 'colored' writer discussing her work and the challenge of being rejected by Africans and whites due to color. As those of us on this side of the world address color and hair issues, I was struck by her insight and moved by the pain she shared. Despite her accomplishments, the issue of color is still very present. How many folks on this side are having this issue without a forum to share and explore it?

A very talented and articulate 13-year-old young lady, Karabo Masimela led the discussion on the life of the great anti-apartheid activist Stephen Biko. She shared with the many children over 30 who attended on a Sunday afternoon. The children were actively engaged and moved by her presentation; comrade Raks arranged for her to share on a radio broadcast. Book club activities would benefit many children on this side; it was very inspiring to see children from a poor community attend and be engaged and aspire to enhance their education; as always, we have overcome the barriers.

During my visit to Thabisile School in Soweto, I met students who were very energetic and excited about meeting folks from this side. As is the case with many schools in poor communities, the need for repair is immense, but in this case, the desire to learn has not been diminished despite the facilities. They are articulate in English in addition to various African languages. Their goals are clear, and they wonder if I know Beyonce lol. Like children everywhere, they are hopeful about their future, and some of their aspirations are shaped by what they see, especially in the media. The Global Literacy Project (GLP) has partnered with the Pingry School to arrange for students to participate in a service-learning project. The students collect books and funds to enhance students' academic opportunities and use the funds to purchase other items to improve school facilities. These efforts should be applauded; it is commendable to assist people. I also hope that we will create opportunities for children of African ancestry to be involved.

Comrade Raks graciously extends an invitation to attend a reception in honor Nadine Gordimer, a South African writer, political activist, and recipient of the 1991 Nobel Prize in Literature, when she was recognized as a woman "who through her magnificent epic writing has significantly contributed to ending apartheid. The Mexican Ambassador is giving her the highest civilian award only two other South Africans have been so honored; Nelson Mandela and Bishop Desmond Tutu. Nadine is moved by the honor and explains how she was destined to use her talent to help shape the world in a humanitarian manner. Some of her invited guests include George Bizos, the lawyer who defended Nelson Mandela during the treason trial. His role in the anti-apartheid struggle was critical. The opportunity to interact with some of the historic fighters for justice is true honor and blessing.

Visiting Robben Island is a sobering reminder of the profound sacrifice made by many ANC members and political prisoners everywhere. The inhumane treatment, beatings, not being allowed to see family members, even the food rations, were issued in a racist manner. Mandela and others strengthen themselves and each other to continue their heroic fight for justice. We, on this side, should learn the lesson of staying connected to our political prisoners.

Aluta Continua...

# Familia

## Photos & Awards

## The Davis Crew

*Mom and Daddy.*

*The Courier News article on our track team win.*

THE COURIER-NEWS, Thursday, June 5, 1969 35

# Maxson Wins Rotary Track Titles

## Flood Nine Posts Win

## Frame Sparks Union Win; Elmore, McCray Triumph

## Metuchen Breezes

*The Courier News track photo.*

*My graduation from Rutgers College, 1976.*

*Father of the Year Award.*

Office of the President
155 MILL ROAD • P.O. BOX 3050 • EDISON, NEW JERSEY 08818-3050
(908) 906-2517 • FAX (908) 494-8244

May 30, 1997

Mr. William Davis
Director
Middlesex County College
New Brunswick Center
317 George Street
New Brunswick, NJ 08901

Dear Bill:

Congratulations on your selection as one of the recipients of the first annual Father's Day Recognition Award. I regret that a prior engagement will preclude my attending the festivities on June 15. I hope that you and your fellow honorees have a wonderful time at the show.

Sincerely,

John Bakum, Ed.D.
President

JB:jcb

*A wonderful opportunity for me and the Crew to appear on Reading Rainbow. See episode on my website.*

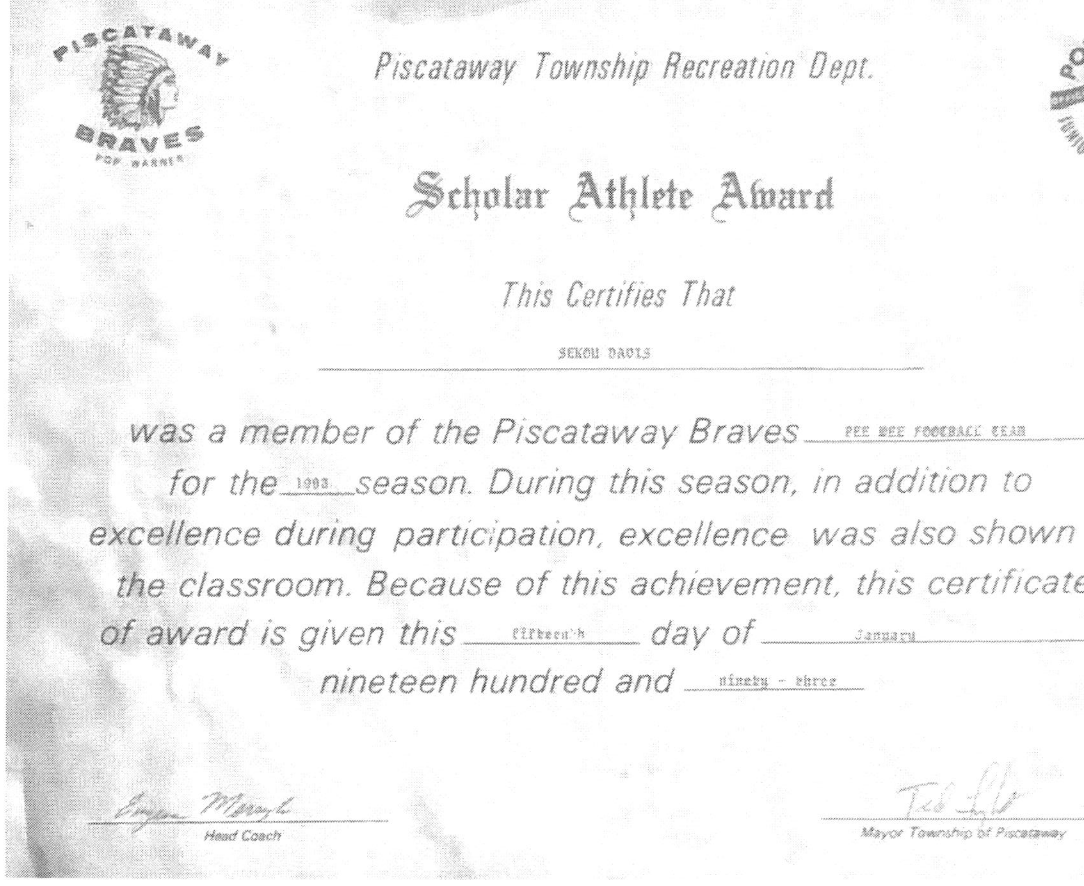

Piscataway Township Recreation Dept.

Scholar Athlete Award

This Certifies That

SEKOU DAVIS

was a member of the Piscataway Braves PEE WEE FOOTBALL TEAM for the 1993 season. During this season, in addition to excellence during participation, excellence was also shown in the classroom. Because of this achievement, this certificate of award is given this fifteenth day of January nineteen hundred and ninety - three

Head Coach

Mayor Township of Piscataway

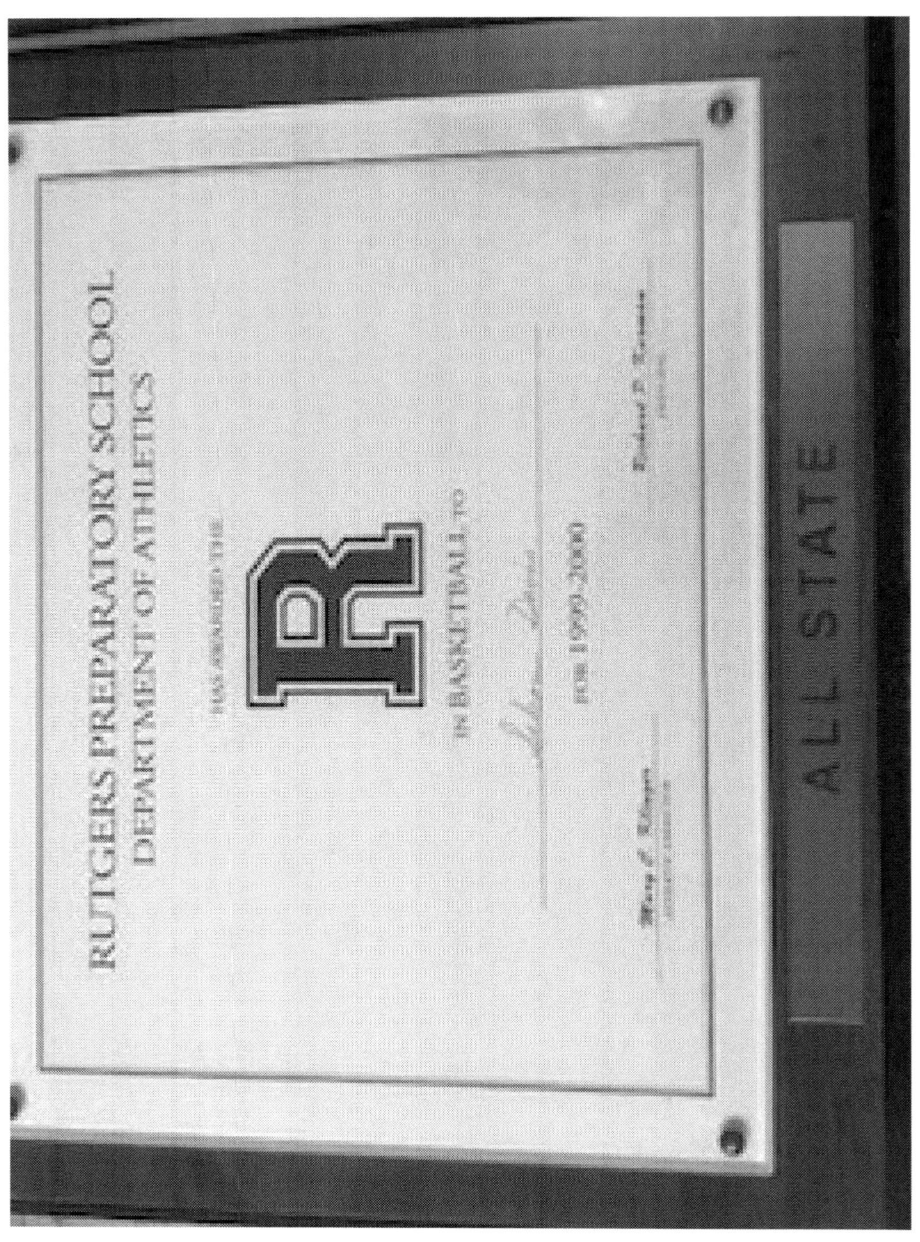
RUTGERS PREPARATORY SCHOOL
DEPARTMENT OF ATHLETICS
R
IN BASKETBALL TO
FOR 1999-2000
ALL STATE

CASSIDY
SPLIT PERSONALITY
RIAA
PRESENTED TO
CASSIDY
SPLIT PERSONALITY
CASSIDY

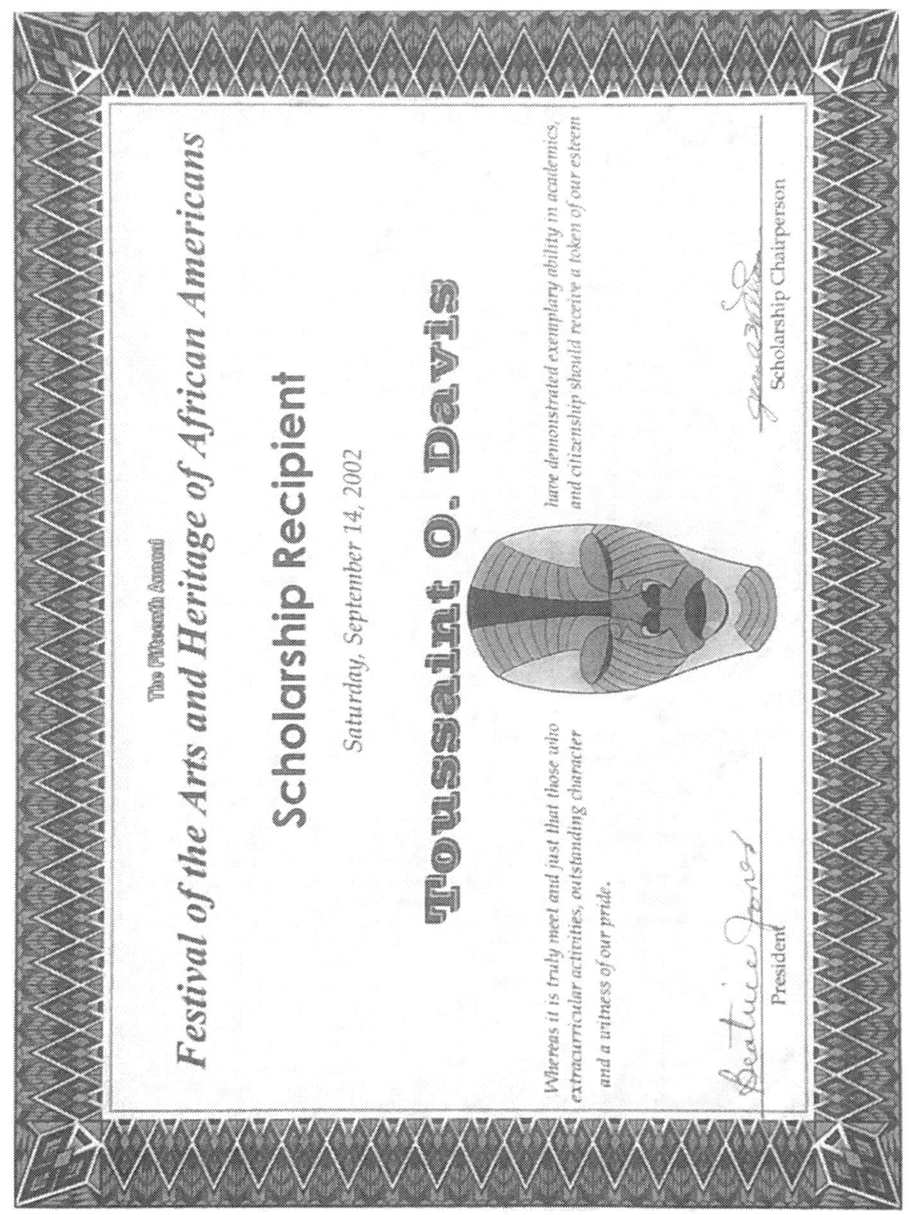

Festival of the Arts and Heritage of African Americans

Scholarship Recipient

Saturday, September 14, 2002

Toussaint O. Davis

Whereas it is truly meet and just that those who have demonstrated exemplary ability in academics, extracurricular activities, outstanding character and citizenship should receive a token of our esteem and a witness of our pride.

President

Scholarship Chairperson

**NEW JERSEY GENERAL ASSEMBLY**

**Joseph V. Egan**
Assemblyman, 17th District
100 Bayard Street
2nd Floor
New Brunswick, NJ 08901
(732) 249-4550
FAX (732) 249-6426
asmegan@njleg.org

**Committees**
Labor
Telecommunications and Utilities
Housing and Local Government

May 14, 2003

Toussaint Davis

Dear Toussaint:

I recently became aware of your Dean's Award for Co-Curriculum Excellence. I wanted to extend my congratulations to you on this distinguished honor. Clearly, you have begun a journey in higher education that will undoubtedly be filled with accomplishments and successes.

The honor of receiving such an award comes only after devotion and hard work, both in the classroom and within the community at large. You should feel great pride that your work was deserving of recognition. As your representative, in the New Jersey General Assembly, I am proud to see you achieve this level of success in your first year at Rutgers.

On behalf of myself, and the residents of the 17th Legislative District of New Jersey, I congratulate you. I wish you the best of luck, both in college and in future endeavors.

Sincerely,

Assemblyman Joseph V. Egan

*Printed on Recycled Paper*

Office of the Dean · Rutgers College
Rutgers, The State University of New Jersey
Milledoler Hall · Room 103
520 George Street · New Brunswick · New Jersey 08901-1167
732/932-7731 · FAX: 732/932-9009

June 29, 2006

Toussaint Davis

Dear Toussaint:

Your fine academic record of the Spring 2006 term has qualified you for inclusion on the Rutgers College Dean's List. You should be proud of this achievement.

We are pleased that you are continuing in the Rutgers tradition of academic excellence. Congratulations on this accomplishment and best wishes for continued success.

Sincerely,

Lenore Neigeborn
Associate Dean

# PISCATAWAY HIGH SCHOOL
*Office of the Principal*

**100 Behmer Road Piscataway, NJ 08854-4173 - (732) 981-0700, ext. 2200 Fax: (732) 562-8670**

Dr. Michael A. Wanko
*Principal*

Robert Copeland
*Superintendent of Schools*

Alix Arvizu, *Assistant Principal*
Avis Clarke, *Assistant Principal*
Ralph Pennacchio, *Assistant Principal*
Carol Przystup, *Assistant Principal*

March 2003

To the Family of
Imani Davis

Dear Parent/Guardian:

Our counseling department recently completed a review of student report cards and I am pleased to inform you that your child has been placed on the High Honor Roll for the 2nd marking period of the 2002-03 school year. The attainment of all As in all courses in which a student is enrolled is truly an honor.

We realize the amount of work and dedication that it takes to attain this degree of accomplishment. We also realize the amount of effort it takes on behalf of the parents to provide an atmosphere conducive to study and to encourage their children to attain the highest possible level of competency in their academic endeavors.

We would like to honor your child and you at a breakfast to take place on Friday, March 21, 2003, in the Patton cafeteria at 8:30 a.m. We look forward to meeting you and your child at that time.

Congratulations and best wishes for continued success.

Sincerely,

M.A. Wanko, PhD.

Michael A. Wanko, Ph.D.
Principal

/jp
M2ndMP02-03

*Scholarship Uplift – "A Vision of Excellence"*

PISCATAWAY
BRAVES
POP WARNER

Piscataway Township Recreation Dept.

Scholar Athlete Award

This Certifies That

IMANI DAVIS

was a member of the Piscataway Braves Junior Pee Wee Cheerleading Squad for the 1996 season. During this season, in addition to excellence during participation, excellence was also shown in the classroom. Because of this achievement, this certificate of award is given this thirteenth day of February nineteen hundred and ninety-seven

Head Coach

Mayor Township of Piscataway

Rutgers

**OUTSTANDING PARENT AWARD**

**RUTGERS, THE STATE UNIVERSITY OF NEW JERSEY**

Takes pleasure in presenting this award of recognition to

*Bill Davis*

as

*Imani Davis*

graduates high school and becomes a recipient of our

**JAMES DICKSON CARR SCHOLARSHIP**

Your support and care in helping to make this day possible is
admirable and highly worthy of praise.

Presented at Rutgers University on this 9th day of April 2005

Dr. Richard L. McCormick
President
Rutgers, The State University of New Jersey

*In the spirit of Umoja (Unity)*

Please join us in celebrating

Imani's

graduation from

*Rutgers University*

and wish her well as she begins her fellowship at

*Johnson & Johnson*

and her

*M.A. at Rutgers*

*Saturday, June 13th*
*3 p.m.*

*Some of Imani's accomplishments:*

Graduating cum laude
High honors in her major
J&J Fellowship
Dean's List
And many more!

*Regrets Only*

*Don't forget your swim suit!*

# Quibbletown Middle School

Piscataway, New Jersey

## Student Achievement Award

*This certifies that*

Imani Davis

has attained 2nd Honor Roll status in the 2nd marking period

2/15/01

Home Room Teacher

Principal

Middlesex County College Child
Care Center Day Camp
Certificate
OF
ACHIEVEMENT
Presented to
Naeemah
For
Best
Journalist
July8-July26, 1996

Piscataway Township Recreation Dept.

POP WARNER OFFICIAL JUNIOR LEAGUE FOOTBALL

# Scholar Athlete Award

This Certifies That

NAEEMAH DAVIS

was a member of the Piscataway Braves Junior Pee Wee Cheerleading Squad for the 1997 season. During this season, in addition to excellence during participation, excellence was also shown in the classroom. Because of this achievement, this certificate of award is given this twelfth day of February nineteen hundred and ninety-eight

Beth Braconi
Head Coach

Mayor Township of Piscataway

PISCATAWAY TOWNSHIP DEPARTMENT OF RECREATION

*Scholar Athlete Award*

This certifies that

NAEEMAH DAVIS

was a participant in the Piscataway Braves Pop Warner Program during the 1999 season. This certificate is presented in recognition of the academic excellence achieved during the Pop Warner season.

presented by Kevin Donovan
Director of Recreation

February 3, 2000

President's Education Awards Program

PRESIDENT'S
AWARD FOR EDUCATIONAL EXCELLENCE

presented to

Naeemah Davis

in recognition of

Outstanding Academic Excellence

2007

U.S. Secretary of Education

President of the United States

Principal

Piscataway High School
School

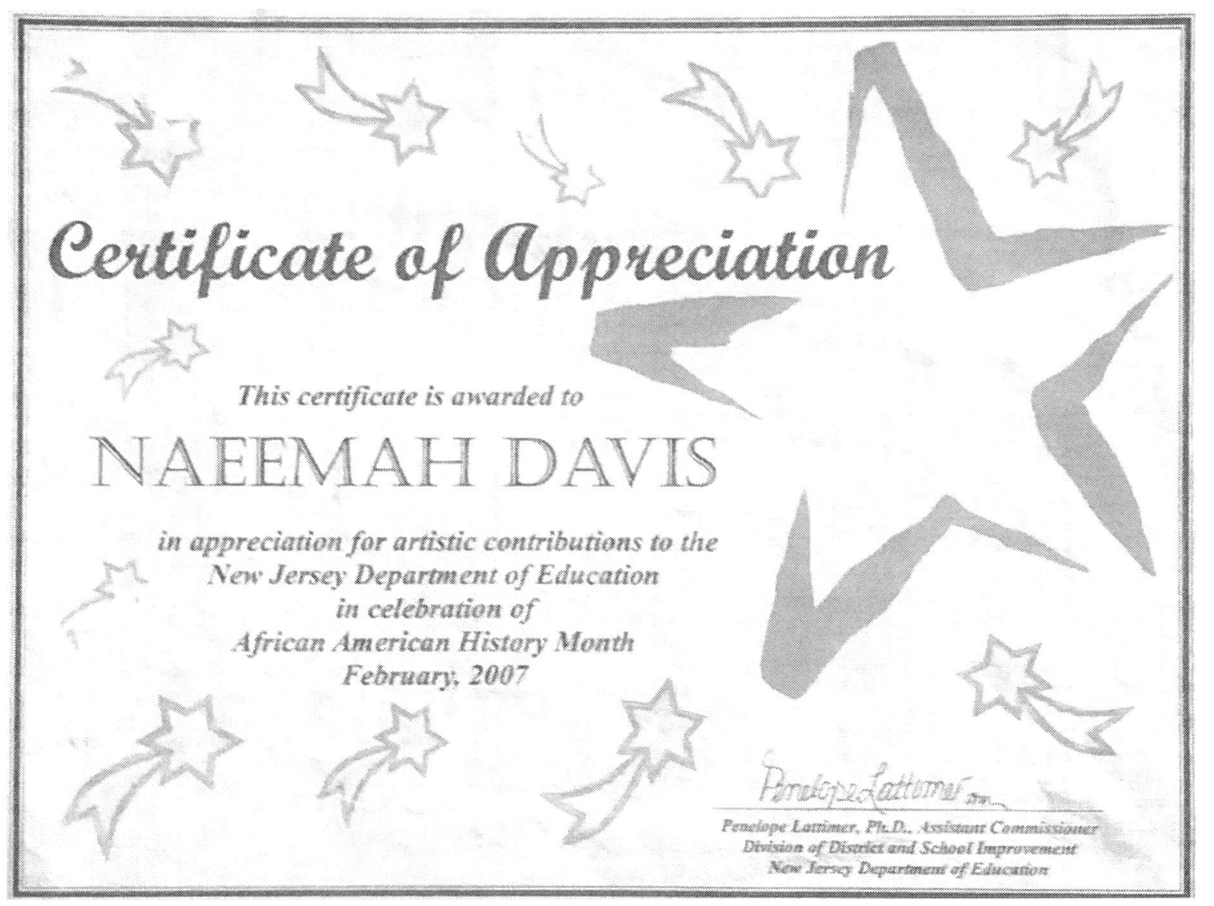

Certificate of Appreciation

This certificate is awarded to

NAEEMAH DAVIS

in appreciation for artistic contributions to the
New Jersey Department of Education
in celebration of
African American History Month
February, 2007

Penelope Lattimer, Ph.D., Assistant Commissioner
Division of District and School Improvement
New Jersey Department of Education

*Marshall, Elijah, Jean, Barbara and me*

*My brother Marshall, nephew Elijah, and me*

***Dedicated to my younger brother Kevin***

***Ode to Kevin ( KBD)—the original Obi-Wan***

The Creator has a master plan
But sometimes we don't understand
It seems my brother left the land
too soon
My brother Kevin recently went to heaven
He left us the other day
He told me to tell everyone hey
He was a good man sometimes hard to understand
He had his own style with a sly smile
Like, mom, he had a lot of fire
Having a debate was one of his greatest Desires
A true Trekkie like daddy the 'Emperor' of the universe

He wanted to make the world a better place
We know he's smiling down on us from Heaven
Rest in peace and power my brother
We love and miss you
*RIP 2015*

*My siblings: Me, Jean, Kevin, Barbara, and Marshall aka the Five Tots*

BABA AND THE CREW

*My 60th Birthday Party Celebration*

*Family vacation 2019, Barbados. I am standing with my aunt Aunt Willa*

# PART III
# Redemption

*"Have a vision of excellence, a dream of success, and work like hell."*
**— Dr. Samuel DuBois Cook**

# CHAPTER 14

# BABA CREW EVALUATIONS

*"Whoever controls the mind of our children controls the future."*
**— Julius Nyerere**

In hindsight, there are times when I am still amazed at how the Crew and I made it this far. One key aspect of our daily lives was consistency. I made sure we ate dinner together every night, with very few exceptions. Everyone knew what to expect at all times, and we settled into our routine despite the obstacles.

My editor suggested that she interview the crew individually and get their take on their upbringing. In her questioning, she asked that none of them share their responses with the other. Honestly, I did not see the responses until I was presented with the final draft. None of the responses were edited as it was necessary to share each person's genuine emotions. The interview starts with Naeemah, the youngest, then Imani, then Toussaint, and last but not least, Sekou, the oldest.

AFRICA

## Naeemah

**Q. Thinking back to your childhood, I saw The Reading Rainbow footage. Describe what that was like? How much time did you have before the show was taped? Did you watch the show prior to the taping? Do you recall anything particular about LeVar Burton? Anything that stands out to you now as an adult and the impact of that episode on the family.**

**A.** I remember the taping happened right around my birthday and everyone on the set was kind. It was exhausting for me - right before the birthday scene was filmed, I believe I had to lay down and take a nap because I was getting too cranky. I don't remember watching the show before or after its release. I recall LeVar Burton being very friendly, and he made an effort to make sure my siblings and I were comfortable. As an adult, the significance is way greater in my eyes. How many shows positively portrayed a single black father raising his children in a healthy way? I remember just a few.

**Q. You all have African names. How did that make you feel growing up? Were you teased? Did you have any classmates with your name? What does your name mean to you as an African American adult?**

**A.** Growing up, when we would go to an event or function as a group, my father would line us up in age order and we would each have to introduce ourselves, including our FULL name and the meaning of it. Imagine being as shy as I was having to say, "My name is Naeemah Ife Safiya Davis and it means benevolent loved one and wise." Needless to say, I did not enjoy this as a child. I don't remember ever getting teased for my name, but some of the teachers had a tough time trying to pronounce it on the first day of school. As diverse as Piscataway was, I never had any classmates with my name as a kid. As an adult now, the uniqueness and history behind my name means a lot more to me. I absolutely love my name more now as an adult, and I would not ever change it.

**Q. Your dad played both roles as father and mother throughout your lives. Were there instances in school, activities, where you felt uncomfortable or awkward because your mom was not present? Did your friends have two parent homes?**

**A.** Thankfully the village Baba built for us really showed up to help out when we needed them. I don't recall ever feeling awkward, but I know at times I felt her absence more than others. When Baba was being extremely strict, I would often wish that she was with us to give him another perspective. My adolescence was particularly tough with all the changes that come with being a teenager. My godmother played a very key role in our lives - she was always there to help in whatever way she could. My god-family's household had both parents (my godparents), two daughters, and a beautiful and super welcoming home just around the corner from our house. It was so critical for me and Baba, because we had some difficult moments during that period. Out of my friend group, it was about equally split with two-parent homes and single-parent homes.

**Q. Did you ever want to run away because you felt your dad was too tough on you?**

**A.** I only had that thought once. I did ask him to send me to boarding school and he let me know in his Baba way that you can't run away from your problems. This was during my teenage phase when I challenged Baba's rules. It was very rough on all of us. Once I went to college, I better understood Baba's mentality on how he raised us and what he was trying to keep us from, and he did a superb job at it. There were aspects of it that I would have done differently as a parent in an effort to create an environment where my children feel comfortable being honest with me as much as possible. My methods of "running away" were sleeping over a friend's house.

**Q. What were some of the adolescent and teenage conflicts that taught you about your dad's character?**

**A.** Sometimes when I reflect on my adolescent and teenage years, it feels like all of it was spent in conflict with Baba but that isn't true. I had a hard time respecting his rules because they were so much stricter than the rules that any of my friends or peers had to follow. There was a period where I was consistently breaking the rules and ending up on punishment. Baba did not waver and that's what I learned about him at that time. He would always tell me "you're going to keep getting the same lesson until you learn it." As an adult, I know that to be true in many scenarios. Baba had two main goals for us at all times - safety and keeping the family together. Everything he did was based on those principles.

Another range of issues began to arise when Imani and I were high school/college age and wanted to socialize more. These issues were internal family issues, because our brothers would get more freedom than us, which contributed to my rebellious behavior. I understand that this was to keep us even more safe, but Baba just could not fully understand what Imani and I were experiencing.

**Q. Describe the household climate when you were teenagers. For example, chores, looking after each other, cooking, homework. Did you have other adults helping out when your dad worked?**

**A.** By the time I was a teenager, all of my siblings were already old enough to watch me and themselves. Chores were literally the same every week and we would rotate the schedule so it was fairly shared. All of us were in a bunch of activities after school so when we would get home it would be time for homework until dinner was ready. Baba made home cooked meals every day. We ate together for dinner every single night, unless someone had a concert or game or something else. And even if that was the case, we would all be there TOGETHER. The Davises were a unit and everyone knew it. The older I got I started to cook more just because I enjoy it and still do. Weekends were usually Baba and I making brunch for everyone. By the time I learned how to make breakfast potatoes, my siblings were waking me up to cook -- and I loved it! Cooking for my family and loved ones has always been a joy of mine.

In terms of school and homework, there was no negotiation about school. It always came first in our household and Baba extended that priority to the community. He started and ran his own tutoring program in Piscataway for many years on Saturday mornings called Epic Vision. Baba would bring his own tutors to PHS Saturday detention and help the students that were there since they couldn't leave either way. Other students were also welcome to join if they needed help, and the whole program was totally free. As someone who struggled continuously with math and science, I would have to go to Epic Vision tutoring on Saturdays at 8am. As a night owl, you could imagine having to wake up that early on a weekend. It was a motivation to get my grades up, because if any of our grades dropped below a B in an academic class, your consequence was going to tutoring on Saturday morning with Baba. Baba never played about school.

**Q. Describe your dad in three words.**

**A.** Disciplined, Hardworking, Intelligent. 4$^{th}$: PRO-BLACK!

**Q. Talk about family traditions that started when you were younger and continue today.**

**A.** Interesting question. Some of them are the same but in a new and more modern version. For example, when we were younger we had family dinner together while everyone lived home. Obviously these days we're all over the country, but we literally check-in with each other every day in our full family chat and then there's a separate chat just for the siblings. It's our way of still keeping in touch when we can't see each other daily. Other traditions that have continued are our annual Kwanzaa celebration, our Family & Friends cookout every summer, celebrating birthdays together every year, and we've really ramped things up since Nia was born. The most important tradition that we learned from childhood was to keep the family first. It was instilled in us and it's the reason we remain so close today.

**Q. What characteristics or other qualities are you like your dad? Good and bad.**

**A.** Baba and I are so similar and it's the reason why we get along so well, and also why we bump heads at times. When I was a child, one of the nicknames Elders would say was Lil Bill because I look just like him, our birthdays are 3 days apart, and I'm basically his twin. Things that we have in common, good and bad, are: confidence, stubbornness, assertiveness, loyalty, hardworking, family focused, pro-Black, politically aware, enjoy cooking, we stand our ground and we are the glue that holds the family together.

**Q. What was your relationship with your mother as a youth, and what is it like today?**

**A.** Until I was in my teenage years, I didn't know a lot about my mother outside of the basics: where she's from, some family history, her modeling career, the split between my parents and her living out of state. My mother is a very reserved person, but she will become more conversational once she's comfortable. Since we unfortunately did not get to spend a lot of time together during my childhood, interactions would be awkward or strained at first when she moved back to New Jersey. But as an adult, what my relationship with my mother has taught me is, it starts with you. I decided a few years ago I was going to put in the work to develop a more meaningful connection with my mother. In my honest opinion, it's been too long already and I should've started a long time ago. Managing my own expectations has helped immensely. In any relationship, the first step is meeting people where they are and being okay with that. It really isn't fair to put your expectations on other people, especially not knowing their full story or history, but most of us do it often. I decided to get to know my mother as a human being first and it has been a very fulfilling journey with her.

**Q. Is there anything you wish your dad did differently in rearing you?**

**A.** As I stated earlier, I would have liked for my father to be less strict and also more fair in the discrepancies between privileges with his sons and daughters. Otherwise, we are a walking testimony of the incredible job Baba did raising us.

**Q. How has your dad helped shape/nurture your career?**

**A.** As a professor, Baba enforced attending a four-year university and getting a degree before wanting to pursue anything else. I remember when I first wanted to go to culinary school after high school, which is not surprising seeing that I'm now in the culinary field professionally. It took some time for me to get here, but I'm a firm believer that everything happens when it's supposed to. And my Rutgers experience gave me so much that I needed to grow into a responsible and high functioning adult. It was the relationships that I built while there that brought me to where I am today. When my opportunity comes to parent, I hope I won't prohibit my children from exploring their dedicated interests.

As an adult, Baba has supported all of my career changes. From education to advertising to entrepreneurship, he's given his support, time and dedication. My whole family has been extremely supportive of my business endeavours. I could not have built what I have without them.

**Q. What mantras do you live by?**

**A.** Family first. Love & loyalty. Stick to your word. Set boundaries and stick by them. Everything happens when it's supposed to. God will keep giving you the same lesson until you learn it. Hard work beats out talent.

**Q. How has Nia changed everyone's life?**

**A.** Nia is one of my favorite people in the universe. She has brought so much joy and happiness to all of our lives, but for some reason I feel like especially mine. Probably because I've always, always loved children. My first career goal was to be an early childhood teacher then open my own daycare. My first job at 12 was at a daycare center. So when we found out Nia was coming I was just thrilled! I was in the room when she was born and I see her as much as I can. She is the most brilliant child, so kind, so generous, so sweet and truly herself.

Nia's birth elevated the family's connection and allowed all of us to evolve as a unit, as well as individually. We see each other as much as possible because it's a joy to be a part of Nia's childhood. She's expressed to Baba before how she knows and understands how much we love her. And just knowing she recognizes that makes me so happy, because she's learning the foundations of how important family is. Sekou has become the most popular family member since he brought us the first grandchild. It's amazing how a child can bring a close family even closer. That's what she's done for us. And finally, she's been an inspiration for all of us, but especially Sekou, to go harder, work harder and achieve even more. Kou has totally turned his life around after Nia was born. It's been amazing to see in real time. We're all so proud of him. #TeamNiaBia

**Q. What things are you planning to do with your own children that were important to you?**

**A.** I want my children to always know and understand that I love and accept the whole person that they are. They will be raised with spiritually guided, family focused principles from day one, the same way we were taught. If God blesses me with more than one child, they will be raised to stick by their siblings as well and that we are a unit - what one person does affects the entire group.

Additionally, I will nurture and support them on their career path and life passions. This is super important to me because I've been on both sides of it, and having your family's support when trying to achieve an unconventional dream is so important.

I plan on raising my children to be a humble, compassionate, loving, financially independent, open-minded, and cultured crew, among many other qualities. They'll be taught their true history as Native people, what that means, and how to move in this world knowing that. They'll be taught about healthy boundaries, respect for themselves and others, the importance of hard work and ROI. And most importantly - through their parents - they'll be taught what it means to be in a healthy, loving relationship, why it's important to be kind, and how to love unconditionally.

**Q. What were some of your most memorable family trips and why? Did you get to choose the location? How were the activities decided? Did you make friends and connect with them afterward? Have you visited any childhood family trips as an adult?**

**A:** Growing up, the trip I remember the most was going to Disney World for New Years Eve in 1999, and then going on a Carnival Cruise to the Bahamas directly afterwards. Baba wanted to be somewhere warm just in case Y2K was really a thing. It was such an amazing time, mainly because it was a complete surprise. I don't know how Baba kept that all under wraps. The second reason is, it's the only cruise I've been on to this day.

We had great family road trips as well, usually to see family. Our late grandmother lived in a very country part of South Carolina and it was always like a new world when we would visit her. She would serve fried fish for breakfast and I, for one, was not complaining.

**Q: Discuss playing dress-up. Did you borrow items from the village of women? :). What female did you aspire to be/look like? What songs did you sing? Dance? How did Baba react? Did you put on shows for him and other family members?**

**A:** I don't remember playing dress-up too much. I really loved Aaliyah when I was growing up. I tried to create her look many times. Also, as a teenager I got really into make-up so I was always trying to imitate a Naomi Campbell or Tyra Banks look. As far as singing, dancing, entertaining the family etc., it wasn't really like that. Imani and I would write and sing songs on a tape recorder but we never debuted it to the family.

**Q: Who were your favorite babysitters/caregivers and why?**

I remember really liking one of our babysitters, because she was younger than our previous ones and she let us get away with some things. She would level with us. And, she gave us chicken! Chicken fingers to be exact. I also loved going to our former Reverend's house. She worked at the church where our step team was based. She was the first one to ever straighten my hair. Something I'll never forget! And of course I loved spending time at my godmother's house.

**Q: Stealing appears to be a theme that Baba mentioned and later all of the crew stole at some point and time. Discuss why the temptation to steal was there despite Baba's stern warnings not to steal. What types of things did you steal? Did your friends encourage stealing? Did Baba uncover stolen items? Were you punished? Discuss any details and dialogue.**

We all had our experiences with theft as children. We learned our lessons the hard way and moved on.

**Q: Baba was suspended from school several times from elementary through high school. Discuss some of your school suspensions: what did you do? How long? How often? Dialogue from Baba or school administrators.**

I never got suspended from school, though I may have gotten detention once or twice. detention one or two times. As far as some of my siblings who did get suspended, I remember their punishments. First thing was, multiply the number of days you were suspended by a week for the duration of your punishment. And it could go up from there if you broke the rules while on punishment. So while they were home suspended they had plenty of chores and work to do. Baba made sure the lesson got learned.

**Q: Your family honors the Paul Robeson legacy as scholars, artists, athletes, and activists. I have general information about your academics and athleticism. Discuss more detail about your artistry and activism. If possible, go back to your younger self to the present day.**

**A.** I've always been drawn to art and creativity. Any opportunity to express my introverted self through non-verbal communication I seized. I was very shy as a child when it came to speaking to new people. Baba would have us out at the rallies early Saturday mornings for whatever injustice was happening at that time, but as a child I didn't truly understand or appreciate the need for this. But I really started to understand art and activism when I got to college, and even more so after I graduated and got out into the world. I still haven't fully figured out how to use my art for activism, but I support people who have. As far as athleticism, health is wealth and it's become much more important to me as an adult to take better care of myself.

**Q: What does this quote mean to you: Julius Nyerere, former President of Tanzania stated, 'Whoever controls the minds of our children will control our future'**

**A:** This is a pretty straightforward quote. I have faith that my generation will correct some of the errors of our predecessors, and the generation that follows mine will have to do the same for us. Unfortunately and fortunately that's just how it goes. I'm really excited to see how Nia's generation will lead. She is so much smarter than we were at her age, and it's because we're raising her somewhat differently than how we were raised. My siblings and I have many resources and we pour everything into her. It's been an incredible investment so far. I look forward to raising my own children for this very reason: raising good people who will help shape the better future this world so desperately needs.

## Imani

**Q. What were some of your most memorable family trips and why? Did you get to choose the location? How were the activities decided? Did you make friends and connect with them afterward? Have you visited any childhood family trips as an adult?**

**A.** We had so many amazing family trips and most of them included a very long drive in our silver Econoline van – the kind of van that had a couch that turned into a bed, a small table (which we of course broke and then instead had a hole in the floor of the van where you could see the street) and a TV. We would go everywhere in that van – to South Jersey to visit our uncles and cousins, to South Carolina to visit Grandma, and to Florida to visit Disney World. There were so many memories in that van: the boys having farting contests and Baba yelling out "If y'all are gonna act like animals, I'm gonna leave you on the side of the road!", naps we took on the back bed and getting carried inside if we were still asleep when we arrived at our destination (sometimes I pretended to be asleep so I would get carried in), listening to Bob Marley, Stevie Wonder, The Sounds of Blackness, and Arrested Development, eating snacks we didn't normally get to eat and playing games. We spent so much time in that van together that those were the times we got closer. It was really special.

I really liked visiting Grandma in South Carolina because it was so much different than where we lived. She lived in a tiny town called Ridgeland where they served pizza (not by the slice) and fried chicken at the gas station. It was the first time I'd seen a Piggly Wiggly (grocery store). Grandma lived in a small mobile home (not a trailer home as she corrected me on this!) near a little lagoon where an alligator also lived. There were lizards and other wildlife all over the place. As kids we just got to play, and it was such a quiet and tiny town that there were no worries about us being outside. I also remember reading her books, which were always about Black people and Black excellence, including the 400 paged *Autobiography of Sammy Davis*, which as a kid, I probably shouldn't have been reading, but added to the allure of visiting her.

**Q. Stealing appears to be a theme that Baba mentioned and later all of the crew stole at some point and time. Discuss why the temptation to steal was there despite Baba's stern warnings not to steal. What types of things did you steal? Did your friends encourage stealing? Did Baba uncover stolen items? Were you punished? Discuss any details and dialogue.**

**A.** I would steal small things like lip gloss or makeup – things that I knew Baba wasn't going to buy and would be pretty easy to steal. I got caught one time at a CVS in New Brunswick. The security guard came around the corner (he had been watching me) right as I was opening a tube of lip gloss and told me to come with him. I followed him to the front of the store where he told me to call my parents. I called my dad's job but instead of talking to him, I talked to his admin and somehow, got her to come down to CVS and pretend to be my aunt so that I wouldn't have to tell Baba. She came and picked me up and we signed some papers. I didn't tell Baba until years later. I knew that if he came, I would be in so much trouble and I just wasn't brave enough to face him. He always said that if we ever got in trouble with the cops or found ourselves in jail not to call him – it was his very direct way of letting us know that this kind of behavior was not acceptable. After getting caught, I never stole again. It was too scary and since I was lucky enough not to get caught by Baba, I didn't want to try it again in case I wasn't so lucky the next time. I always felt terrible when I disappointed Baba!

**Q. Baba was suspended from school several times from elementary through high school. Discuss some of your school suspensions: what did you do? How long? How often? Dialogue from Baba or school administrators.**

**A.** I got suspended twice. Once in middle school and once in high school. Both times for fighting boys. I was never afraid to stick up for myself, something I learned from Baba!

In middle school I got suspended for fighting a classmate because he threw a basketball at my face in the hallway. I had just received a really good grade and was in a great mood, but this perceived disrespect set me into a rage! I immediately lunged at him and scratched his face and we ended up in a physical altercation. Any time I got in trouble the administrators were pretty surprised at me because I was the "golden child" – President of Student Government, on honor roll, in honors classes, etc. Usually, when something like this happened Baba would want to get down to the root of the issue and would host a meeting with the other parents and students involved to make sure nothing like this would happen again. I'm sure he was disappointed, but since I wasn't the aggressor and I was defending myself against a boy, I don't recall getting in too much trouble. I do remember being sad that I was going to miss the 8th grade boat cruise. It was the end of the school year, so my three-day suspension would mean I would miss some of the end of year events.

The high school suspension happened because of an altercation on the after school bus. It was a strange situation where I think I was just trying to be funny, but the situation escalated and a bunch of us got in trouble for bullying, if my memory serves me correctly. Baba implored the school to host a town hall meeting about the incident with all of the students who were involved, as well as their parents. We had to talk about the incident and apologize to our classmate. I'm sure I was on a long punishment for this one, and I never got suspended again.

**Q. Your family honors the Paul Robeson legacy as scholars, artists, athletes, and activists. I have general information about your academics and athleticism. Discuss more detail about your artistry and activism. If possible, go back to your younger self to the present day.**

**A.** I was definitely a scholar, athlete and somewhat of an activist, though I didn't have the artistic gene the same way that Naeemah and Sekou did. Growing up, we always attended protests, marches, and rallies against police brutality and injustice, the same kinds of events that are still taking place today. Baba also made sure we understood Black history, and all of the struggles that our ancestors faced. I think that this is where my sense of activism was derived – I would always speak up for what was right, even if it wasn't popular. I've always believed in justice and fairness as core beliefs.

For me, activism also means challenging social norms and creating a brand-new narrative. I always pursued leadership roles and was elected Student Government President throughout middle and high school. These roles gave me an opportunity to challenge negative stereotypes about young, black women and change the narrative about what we could accomplish, as I had opportunities to work with school administration and influence school policies and even hiring decisions.

This new definition of activism served me well as I continued to serve in leadership roles in undergraduate and graduate school, and this thinking ultimately became a major influence in why I sought a career in Corporate America. As companies have an outsized role in society, it's important for people who look like us to have a seat at the table – it enables us to change the narrative about Black professionals, create pathways for people who look like us, and create the change we want to see from within. I was fortunate to be a part of organizations like INROADS and MLT that are also a part of this important work.

I truly believe that anyone can be an activist by using the platform that they have to create the change that they want to see – whether through art, music, business, or in the traditional sense of advocacy and policy.

**Q. Thinking back to your childhood, I saw The Reading Rainbow footage. Describe what that was like? How much time did you have before the show was taped? Did you watch the show before the taping? Do you recall anything particular about LeVar Burton? Anything that stands out to you now as an adult and the impact of that episode on the family.**

**A.** We always watched the show growing up – it was one of the few shows Baba liked for us to watch as it was educational in nature. That's why it was so cool to meet LeVar – he was a huge celebrity in my mind.

I was about 9 years old at the time, so I don't think I had a real grasp on what any of it meant. For me, it was just a fun experience to talk about what it was like growing up with Baba and my siblings.

In hindsight, our appearance on the show was a huge testament to Baba's vision and what he was already accomplishing as a single, Black father. It allowed him to create a new narrative around single parenthood, which is normally told through the lens of the mother. It feels like it was an early accolade and precursor of what was to come for him as a single father and us as a family.

**Q. You all have African names. How did that make you feel growing up? Were you teased? Did you have any classmates with your name? What does your name mean to you as an African American adult?**

**A.** "Imani means faith – I was named after the seventh principle of Kwanzaa." This is how Baba taught me to introduce myself to everyone when we were growing up. We all had to understand the importance of and meaning behind our names and be ready to share it with others. Over time, I actually enjoyed introducing myself in this manner as it instilled confidence and made me proud of the heritage of my name. People always complimented me on my name, telling me that it was beautiful, which I think is partially because it was unique. At the time, I don't think I fully grasped why Baba made us introduce ourselves in this way, but as an adult I can appreciate how it showed respect and deference to our elders and created pride around me and my siblings' names. People were always impressed when we introduced ourselves in this manner!

**Q. Your dad played both roles as father and mother throughout your lives. Were there instances in school, activities, where you felt uncomfortable or awkward because your mom was not present? Did your friends have two parent homes?**

**A.** In elementary school, my best friend was only raised by her mom. One reason I gravitated toward her was because we had similar situations growing up with one parent and multiple siblings. Seeing other people with just one parent normalized just having Baba for me.

Baba made sure we had strong women role models and went out of his way to cultivate these relationships for us. There were always opportunities for us to learn from and hang out with strong, Black women from our community; which helped to fill the void. Like Naeemah, I also had a godmother and god sister, which gave me another woman to confide in and learn from.

I never felt like it was a weird thing for Baba to be raising us – he created so many norms and so much structure, that it just seemed like it made sense. No one thought he could do it, but he did!

**Q. Describe the household climate when you were teenagers. For example, chores, looking after each other, cooking, homework. Did you have other adults helping out when your dad worked?**

**A.** By the time we were in adolescence, our schedule and structure were really solidified, and we had our system down pact. Every morning, as we ate breakfast together, Baba would start making dinner so that when we got home after all of our activities we could eat together as a family. After school all of us had different activities: marching band, cheerleading, soccer, and basketball, to name a few. Dinnertime was sacred: Baba always had music playing in the background, but there was no TV. Instead, we talked about our days and what was going on at school or in life.

One example of the structure that Baba put in place was having the same dinner menu each week – this allowed him to focus on us and our many activities instead of what we were going to eat. I still remember the menu: Monday we had pasta with red sauce, tacos on Tuesday (my favorite), leftovers on Wednesdays, spinach or tuna pie on Thursday, and homemade pizza with sauce and the tiniest amount of cheese on Friday. Since we had more time on Sunday, we had more of a feast featuring fish and various side dishes. We also got to have Sunday brunch, which was a real treat!

Saturdays were also structured, but we had more time to relax and play. First, we all did our chores, then after we played board games and watched Saturday morning cartoons and shows. I still remember my chore schedule: I had to clean the downstairs bathroom, the stairs, my room and the dining room.

This structure was important as it gave us more time together, doing everything as a family unit. It helped make us as close as we are today. The Reading Rainbow episode did a great job representing our real life!

**Q. Describe your dad in three words.**

**A.** Powerful, Sacrifice, Visionary

**Q. What characteristics or other qualities are you like your dad? Good and bad.**

**A.** We are both headstrong, stubborn, outgoing, and of the world/cosmopolitan. We both care deeply about different cultures and are empathetic. One thing that Baba and I have in common is that we love to talk, and we can talk to anyone! I remember growing up and going to the supermarket with him, he would engage with everyone: cashiers, managers, and even other shoppers – everyone knew him. At the time, it drove me crazy but I now understand that it taught me how to engage with and have respect for people of all walks of life.

**Q. How has your dad helped shape/nurture your career?**

**A.** Baba showed us through his actions what it meant to work hard and not give up on our goals, which definitely shaped how I approached my education and career. Excellence was the expectation that we all lived by.

Because of Baba's example, I graduated cum laude with honors from Rutgers, followed by a Master's degree and a 4.0 GPA also from Rutgers, and finally an MBA and fellowship from Michigan. None of this success would have been possible without the early examples and lessons I learned from Baba.

Although Baba doesn't know everything about the business world or my career, he continues to support my work and development by supporting me in the way he always has – by being there. Whether helping me move to Ann Arbor, across the country to Portland, or listening to me discuss whatever changes are happening in my company, Baba always supports me, reminding me of the values we grew up with – hard work, excellence, and remaining true to myself.

**Q. What mantras do you live by?**

**A.** I still live by the values that we grew up with. Family first, family over everything. Striving for excellence. Being authentic to myself and recognizing what it means to be a Black woman in this world and not compromising who I am, even if it makes other people feel uncomfortable. Believing that I can achieve any goal that I set my mind to. And finally, making sure that I'm reaching back and helping others on a similar path, acting as a guide as Baba has done as an educator.

**Q. How has Nia changed everyone's life?**

**A.** Oh my God, what a wonderful little girl!!! Nia is truly a gift to our family. Sekou was not centered before Nia was born. He lived a fast life centered around parties and the entertainment industry, but her birth helped him to get back on track, realize what was most important, and gave him a new sense of purpose, which is the meaning of her name.

She also helped bring all of us even closer together since we all wanted to spend time with her and support in any way that we could. Nia helped to reinforce our family bond. Watching her grow and learn has also reminded us of the lessons we all learned growing up – I'm sure Sekou is taking a few pages out of Baba's playbook these days!

## Toussaint

**Q. Thinking back to your childhood, I saw The Reading Rainbow footage. Describe what that was like? How much time did you have before the show was taped? Did you watch the show prior to the taping? Do you recall anything particular about LeVar Burton? Anything that stands out to you now as an adult and the impact of that episode on the family.**

The Reading Rainbow experience was surreal. Growing up, I was always a bit shy and suffered from a stutter, so being on television was downright terrifying. I was around 11 or 12 at the time, so the thought of some of my classmates seeing it and teasing me about it added an extra heaping of nerves on top. What I remember more than anything else was how emotional it was for me. In spite of my trepidation, I thought I was doing a reasonably good job of keeping my emotions in check until they asked me "when do you miss your mom the most?" This might have been the first time I can remember having to admit, to a stranger no less, how deeply I missed my mother. I broke down crying and we had to shoot multiple takes because I didn't get through it at first. I'm still not sure how they edited it for clarity, but when you watch it now, it's just my voice and I'm not on screen when talking about it. The producers and my family were really supportive. I know my sisters weren't shy about talking about how much they missed her, so maybe this helped me turn a corner and be okay with the point of missing her.

My father, naturally, was watching the whole time. I've always wondered how it affected him watching me break down repeatedly. I'm sure it wasn't easy. Watching it now, it's more funny than anything else. The hyper stylized nature of the production and the smoothness of our day-to-day was definitely made for TV. Most mornings were a scramble to make sure we were all where we needed to be. The gentle wake-ups and conversation at breakfast depicted on the show were actually admonishments of how close you were cutting it to missing your bus if you didn't get out the house on time. Also, somehow, he woke up with a perfectly symmetrical afro; the magic of television.

Looking back all these years later, what stands out more than anything else is just how young my father looks. He was around 41 or 42 at the time wholly responsible for all of us and having to perform at a high level at work as the sole source of income. I still can't fathom how much of a Herculean effort it took to make sure we were on task daily, His day started at 6am and wasn't over until around 9:30/10pm and his only time to himself was his commute. It's just remarkable he was able to do that everyday with no help.

**Q. You all have African names. How did that make you feel growing up? Were you teased? Did you have any classmates with your name? What does your name mean to you as an African American adult?**

To be honest, I hated my name growing up. The historical significance was never lost on me, but as a self-conscious child, being different meant you attracted unwanted attention. No one I knew was named Toussaint, so it was an easy target to be teased. With the benefit of hindsight, some of those jokes were actually pretty clever…but it doesn't feel that way in the moment. The most popular ones were "Two-ssaint, Three-ssaint, Four-ssaint" (see! clever!) and "Toucan Sam" (less clever).

I was a very skinny kid so I wanted my name to sound tougher. Unfortunately, 12-year-old kids could care less about a history lesson on how Toussaint L'Overture was a legit badass. I told my father once I was going to change my name to Tyrone to achieve the machismo I desired. Thankfully, he laughed it off; thankfully, I grew up.

As an adult, I'm immensely proud of my name and my father's vision to have us understand our history. His own upbringing and studies taught him that as Black Americans, our formal education on where we come is limited to a few days a month when we learn about Martin Luther King and Rosa Parks. Our history is so much richer. By entrusting us with powerful names, the simple act of introducing yourself was a reminder of the greatness of those that came before. That hasn't been lost on me.

**Q. Your dad played both roles as father and mother throughout your lives. Were there instances in school, activities, where you felt uncomfortable or awkward because your mom was not present? Did your friends have two parent homes?**

Around Mother's Day was always challenging for me. It wasn't a discomfort as much as it was a longing for my mother to be around to share some of the experiences with. We'd make cards in school or have moms come visit and that would be sad for me because she wasn't there. I don't ever remember feeling less than my peers because of this. In fact, growing up in a single-parent home, unfortunately, wasn't particularly unique amongst my friends. A lot of my friends in middle and high school had similar circumstances or their parents had remarried. What stood out, however, was how close my father and I were, especially as I go older. I really think my friends admired that relationship and felt a closeness with my father as a result. I still don't know how Baba was able to make it to all of our concerts and most of our sporting events, but he did. At times he was TOO present. Everyone knew when he was in the stands as he was not afraid of speaking his mind. If the referee made an obvious bad call, one of his go-to lines was "C'mon ref! Ray Charles saw that was a foul!!" That was always a crowd favorite.

**Q. Did you ever want to run away because you felt your dad was too tough on you?**

I never threatened to run away, but without thinking through all the consequences, I did write a letter to him once telling him I was going to hurt myself because I was ashamed of my academic performance. To his credit, he addressed it fairly head on and told me that it was unacceptable and I had to step up and do better. Instead of coddling, he sensed I needed someone to believe in me, so pushed to embrace the challenges I faced. I'm not sure how I'd handle it as a parent, or if I think he would have handled it the same way for all of my siblings. His ability to identify what worked best for us as individuals was, ultimately, how he got us to be successful. In hindsight, I just needed to be heard as I felt I was in the giant shadows of my siblings: Sekou was a scholar athlete and talented musician; Imani was an academic superstar striving for perfection; Naeemah was the baby that could do no wrong. I felt a bit rudderless and lost with no identity of my own. It was important for me to understand that charting my own course didn't mean I had to do something drastic, I just had to do it my way and he helped me find it.

**Q. What were some of the adolescent and teenage conflicts that taught you about your dad's character?**

I've always enjoyed a more open relationship with my father than most as we have been able to talk about almost anything without him losing his cool. This may be a bit too personal, but the first time I had sex, the girl told me she was pregnant. This wasn't until very early senior year of high school (September/October) and my best friend threw a house party where it happened. A few weeks later she tells me she's pregnant.

Mind you, I'm still 16 at the time, all I can think about is college and the surrounding pressure of those decisions. On top of that, given my father's experience as a teenage parent, he'd always made it very clear to us his opposition to us repeating his missteps. We were driving home from basketball practice and I had been keeping it in for the better part of three weeks and it was just weighing on me. I didn't want to feel his ire and disappointment, I didn't want to be a parent, I didn't want to put my college dreams on hold. We stopped at a red light and I blurted it out. He waited a beat. And asked me a series of questions about using protection and if anything faltered. I told him it hadn't. He took a deep breath and said, "Well, we'll handle it in due time" and left it there. That was a huge turning point in our relationship where I felt like no matter the challenge we would tackle it as a family.

As I've gotten older, I've continued to be open with him about my relationships with women and what I want. In turn, he's told me some of the complexities with his marriage and relationships since. I'm confident this will always be an anchor for us and will only grow stronger as I start a family.

**Q. Describe the household climate when you were teenagers. For example, chores, looking after each other, cooking, homework. Did you have other adults helping out when your dad worked?**

We've always built our family on the concept of "a village", so there were always adults around the house and neighborhood helping out on chores, tutoring, lending a ride, etc. I truly feel that Baba's energy was infectious in this way. Other parents would see how hard he was working and how committed he was to our academics and extracurricular activities and want to chip in. What also helped was that we lived in a few different neighborhoods in Piscataway, so we kept good relationships across town. Baba was never afraid to get his hands dirty, and we couldn't afford to get a lot of things done professionally. So, when we moved houses, for example, it would be a Baba & The Crew feat. The Uncles production. If he decided he wanted to upgrade the bathrooms, he'd somehow know someone in the neighborhood who had that particular skill-set. The day to day chores rotated. We'd all have to do our fair share of laundry, dishes, cleaning, etc. With respect to outdoor chores, Sekou and I would cut the grass, but we'd all have to rake leaves, shovel snow, pull weeds, help paint and clean the pool. Baba was an equal opportunity distributor of work.

**Q. Describe your dad in three words.**

Present, devoted, determined.

**Q. Talk about family traditions that started when you were younger and continue today.**

Our traditions have always centered around our family - immediate and extended. When we were younger, we'd celebrate both Christmas and Kwanzaa, in addition to having birthday parties and BBQ's in the summer. Now that we're older and living apart, the celebrations are the same, albeit with a bit less fanfare. We still celebrate each other's birthday, usually with a family dinner. Thanksgiving is still the holiday where we see the majority of our immediate family in New Jersey/NY. For the fast several years, it has been either at our house or my Aunt Jean's house. The larger, more community based, festivities are the annual summer BBQ and our Kwanzaa party, both of which we host at the house. As we've gotten older the demographics of these events changed. As kids, we'd have to carefully pick our friends, maybe barter amongst each other for more spots to ensure we included everyone. Kwanzaa especially as there was less space. Now that we've all moved and our friends are more spread out, it is more of Baba's friends and parents who were part of our village. Loud children and video games have been replaced with pressing community and family issues. One of the traditions of the Kwanzaa celebrations is that we go around the room, introduce ourselves and tell the community what you've accomplished in the past year and what your goals are for the upcoming year. As children, it would be some variation of "I was on the honor roll and I plan to do that again". The past few years, however, as members of the village have gotten older and faced significant personal challenges, this opportunity to talk amongst your peers and family carries more weight. I've really admired how people find solace in talking in an environment where they don't feel judged and someone who knows them personally is actively engaged in finding a solution.

**Q. What characteristics or other qualities are you like your dad? Good and bad.**

More than I think I knew, I'm very much like my father and it becomes increasingly apparent the older I get. We align most closely on our hobbies and interests: we're both conscious of our diet and physical fitness, we're both avid readers - global politics is something we can always find time to discuss. I've been blessed with his strong moral compass and sense of justice: we both fall on the side of underrepresented and forgotten. In terms of personality, we're equally good natured and social without needing to be the center of attention, but he's a more natural leader than me. He and Imani are alike in that respect; they have a natural inclination to lead and people are drawn to that magnetism. My father and I are both very patient. While I can't say he was always this way, or it was a function of chasing around four children, I've inherited a longer-term approach and that's driven how I think about the "big" decisions in my life, be it relationships, career, etc. More than anything else, I think we're both fiercely loyal. The way he loves his family and very close friends, is a trait I'm blessed to have developed. The challenge, at times, is learning to understand and live with the disappointment that comes with loving someone. He told me once, "just because someone doesn't love you how you want, doesn't mean they don't love you with all they have." I think about that often, especially as I reflect upon my relationship with my mother.

I've also inherited his competitiveness. We try not to play cards or anything else that pits us against one another as we both like to talk to take the other person off their game. It's all good natured, but we both have pretty loud voices, so it may sound a bit more intense than we intended. We also both have a bad habit of thinking we're right more often than not. We like to hear ourselves talk at times, so learning to listen is something that we can both do better.

**Q. What was your relationship like with your mother as a youth, and what is it like today?**

My relationship with my mother has always been complicated. As a youth, I just couldn't comprehend why my parents weren't together. To me, nothing "happened", so I would hope that maybe they would reconsider and get back together. For whatever reason, it always seemed plausible. Sure, there was distance, but it was something they could fix, if they really tried. I don't think I ever really resented her for not being there, it just made me sad. You'd want to make your mom Mother's Day or Valentine's Day cards. You'd want your mom to come on the class trips as a chaperone. All of those feelings were natural, so I was hopelessly stuck on the idea that there was a slim chance we'd be able to make it right.

As a teenager and young adult, I think I hardened a bit, and I regret taking that stance. I adopted the "with me or against me" mentality, which I'm sure hurt her more than I knew. It wasn't fair to treat her as if she made a decision that she didn't want to be part of our lives. That simply wasn't true. We would be cordial to one another, but I wasn't as warm and loving as I should have been. Baba, to his credit, recognized this and would try to tell me more about their separation and the underlying circumstances. That helped me develop more sympathy and be more open minded and loving.

Even today, our relationship isn't perfect, and I need to continue to push myself to be more actively involved. It hasn't always been easy, but it's improving. It's easy to fall back on what is familiar and easy, but in order to develop and sustain a meaningful relationship, we have to push past history and meet each other where we are now.

**Q. Is there anything you wish your dad did differently in rearing you?**

Every man, at one point or another, thinks he was more talented athletically than he was. I'm no different. While I was a late bloomer in terms of my height and weight, I still think I could've been a better athlete had he pushed me a bit more. He encouraged sports, but they were always a privilege that was granted as long as you were on honor roll, staying out of trouble, etc. I was a good basketball player, but never great, but that doesn't stop me from imagining a world with more guidance and one-on-one coaching. I could've been great. Again, that's not on my father solely. I liked basketball as much as I liked reading, so it all worked out the way it was supposed. to. The priority in our house was academia first, second and third and as much as I'd like to think differently, chances are I'm more successful on my current trajectory than I would've been pursuing sports.

**Q. How has your dad helped shape/nurture your career?**

I've always appreciated that Baba didn't try to dissuade me from pursuing a career in finance. If anything, he knew this wasn't his area of expertise and would try to connect with me with people he thought would be instrumental to my success. There would be times he would see some of the stories around the subprime mortgage crisis he'd, rightly, be uneasy with the role that investment banking played in collapsing the economy especially as it ravaged the Black community. I could only assure him that I wouldn't sacrifice my morals for my career.

What I've learned from him was his willingness to engage in any conversation and his capacity to listen. What has helped me become successful in my career is approaching my business with a long view and deep level of sincerity that I think my clients appreciate. They recognize I'm as interested in maintaining a long, mutually beneficial relationship and I think his affable, open nature is something I've adopted and bring with me to work.

**Q. What mantras do you live by?**

A song that would be on repeat in our house was Sly & The Family Stone's "Family Affair." A line that always stayed with me was "blood is thicker than the mud". To me, his crowning achievement isn't raising us and making sure we're smart, healthy and successful. More importantly, he raised us to understand the value of family, the true spirit of unity. My siblings and I would do anything for one another. In turn, we all know the incredible sacrifices our father made for us and we do everything we can to show him we understand and appreciate it. There isn't an ask that's too big or too small. We're all present in each other's life to an extraordinary degree. We talk everyday, we FaceTime when we feel like it, we joke, we laugh, we're inclusive, we're supportive. When someone meets one of us, they meet all of us. I didn't realize that wasn't the norm until much later life, but I wouldn't change it for the world.

**Q. How has Nia changed everyone's life?**

Her birth has been the single most important event to impact all of our lives over the past six years. It's brought us all closer in ways we probably didn't imagine. We always had an open and honest relationship, though I was probably a bit more withdrawn than everyone else. In order to make sure she's comfortable and happy we all needed to contribute however we could. Her joy is something that makes all of us smile and I know she feels it. To reinforce the message, every time I see her, I tell her "Don't forget Nia, Uncle Tou has your back. Always remember that." This past Thanksgiving, after drilling it into her I stopped and asked if she knew what I meant by it. She took a beat, looked me in the eye and said "I think it means you care for me a lot."

I know she feels that from all of us which is a testament to how Sekou has allowed us to be present in her growth and development.

**Q. What things are you planning to do with your own children that were important to you?**

I want my children to be proud of who they are and what our family represents. I want them to be grounded, open minded and worldly. I want them to know who their parents and grandparents are and their stories: good and bad. And I want them to respect and honor traditions that keep our family close. We can only work towards a future that is brighter than our past. That would mean children who are better, more understanding and open, less judgmental and reserved. I'd want for my children to know their aunts and uncles, appreciate their singular journeys and our collective mission. I'd want my children to revere my father and recognize everything he did was for us.

## Sekou

**Q. Thinking back to your childhood, I saw The Reading Rainbow footage. Describe what that was like? How much time did you have before the show was taped? Did you watch the show before the taping? Do you recall anything particular about LeVar Burton? Anything that stands out to you now as an adult and the impact of that episode on the family.**

**A.** If I remember correctly that was 95-96, I was in 8th grade, and we moved to Piscataway from Newark. Yeah, that clip is funny after getting your email and thinking about it. The things I really remember the most is the production of what it meant to be on TV. A guy came to our house initially and scouted the place. They rearranged things. He said, "OK, there's too much going on in the kitchen. You have too many items out. We have to make it look like a TV kitchen." We rehearsed sitting down at the table and everything else. Going to the local ShopRite was cool because we were able to get things that Baba would not let us have like cereal with sugar. I guess they had it as part of their budget because they just paid for all of our groceries, which was incredible. Watching the show now brought back the memories of how structured those years were. We had the same morning routine. We had the same breakfast of toast, cereal, and fruit, and we had the same dinners on the same day. I watched that episode of Reading Rainbow with Nia, and she recognized me. "That's you da da," she said, pointing to the screen. I try to implement some of the things that my dad taught me in the house.

There was no sugary stuff in the house. Breakfast was cornflakes and honey. At the store, we were trying to get him to buy Lucky Charms like what our friends were having. His middle ground was Kix, and it was a sweet corn cereal, then Berry Kix came out, and we were very happy. A large part of our diet was vegetarian, like Baba, so he limited junk and sugar in the house. Our snacks were fruits and vegetables. Our dinner routine: Mondays there was pasta. Tuesday was Tacos. Thursday may be a spinach pie, and Friday was pizza. Baba had everything down to a science. He knew exactly what he wanted to do and what was going on. There wasn't a lot of room for negotiation. After school, we attended our activities and then did our homework. I rode my bike to school, and my sisters took the bus. It was rinse and repeat for the next day. Thinking back, it kind of made sense to have that type of structure with the responsibility of raising four kids on his own.

Lunchtime was a little embarrassing because we took our lunch to school. It was something healthy. Most kids were buying lunch of a burger and fries, and I had a tuna sandwich. Sometimes on Friday's I could use my allowance and buy a pizza. Allowance was $5 a week.

No one was exempt from work or chores. Every Saturday, everyone got up and did chores. I might do the bathroom and rooms. Each night we rotate who did dishes—vacuuming, sweeping, and cleaning what needed to be cleaned. Before we got to do anything like going outside playing with friends, nothing happened until the house was straight. Again, Baba did not leave any room for negotiations. Dad's rules were pretty much law. As the oldest, I tested those rules the most. I challenged him *all* the time. I always thought I was one step ahead and not very crafty. Challenged the whole dynamic of his structure. I will try to do it my way and see if I can get around doing it your way. There were so many times when I had to come in from playing at a certain time, and I would be out with my friends and joyriding around Piscataway. None of my friends had parents with Baba's type of restrictions. My friends Calvin and Kiel from 5th and 6th grade were raised by mom and grandmom and had a lot of freedom. I just wanted to run around and have fun. There were a bunch of times I was out doing something I was not supposed to do. Then I would be in the room telling my brother I was out doing this and that and my dad could hear in the next room.

One time my friends and I were riding our bikes in a vacant lot in Piscataway. We started throwing rocks and breaking windows. Two white cops came, and it was my first interaction with the police. They were telling us through the megaphone to come out building. My friends rode away. My instinct was to get on my bike and ride away, but I was too scared. Baba came to pick me up. It was one of the worst beatings I got. Baba did not believe in "time out." He always said he would rather it be him beating me than the police.

Baba always talked to me about changing my circle of friends, but I didn't listen. I had another group of friends who were into shoplifting. We took candy, food, anything. My brother was less risky, and he would be with me, his big brother, but never really in the mix. Toussaint had more sense than me. One time we were at Walmart, and we decided to steal the WuTang CD. We had scissors and cut it open, and my friend put it in his jacket. As we were walking out security grabbed him. Toussaint and I looked back, and he yelled out to us, "Call my mother!" Now I had to tell his dad and his mom. It became clear that I needed new friends. I realized I was doing things that were not going to help me go where I want to go. Friends are either going to bring you up or down. If you see your circle changing, you have to change your circle. I took heed to that and moved through certain circles who were doing the same things since I wanted to play basketball and go to college. I see how some of those guys I hung out with are in and out of jail and still getting their lives together. All of the things my dad was preaching were definitely true.

**Q. Your dad raised you as a vegetarian. Do you still have the same eating habits?**

**A.** I have a more modern take on what we are doing. I am more pescatarian, and we eat fish but not turkey, pork, or chicken. I tell people we are not vegetarian but pescatarian. I used to do meatless Mondays, and I was really good, not tempted until I went to college at Hampton University. There was no way for me to survive college without chicken! I needed to bulk up for weight training and tried burgers, but I had to give that up. Nia is a pescatarian. Very rarely, she will have a little chicken. Most meals we cook here are vegetarian with fish.

**Q. You all have African names. How did that make you feel growing up? Were you teased? Did you have any classmates with your name? What does your name mean to you as an African American adult?**

**A.** I have heard every instance of pronouncing Sekou. Most usually say "Sekow," or they just could not get it. I was not teased. I always had a nickname. My black friends called me "Kou," and my white friends called me "Sey." In the band and in the drumline, they called me Sey. It has been impossible for me to get others to pronounce my name. Even in college graduation, you have to write it phonetically, and they still did not get it right. I don't think any teacher ever got it right, either.

Very early on, we all had to know what our names meant and who we were in honor of. Whenever we were out, and my dad introduced us to people and stood in line and say our full name and meaning.

**What characteristics or other qualities are you like your dad? Good and bad.**

I think I can attribute my social personality to my dad. Seeing him as a kid just walk up to anyone and begin a conversation was always fascinating. Plus, everywhere we went, someone always walked up and knew who he was. I learned a lot of that from him. I guess the saying "the apple doesn't fall far from the tree" would also apply to my mischievous childhood ways. I seemed to inherit that from him as well lol. One year for Kwanzaa, I was still working on my music career, and I did not have enough money to purchase him a gift. I decided to produce a song for him. I had all of my siblings come to my studio, and we recorded a version of Tupac's "Dear Mama," and we made it "Dear Baba." The lyrics I wrote really capture how I feel about him and everything he has done for the four of us.

**Q. What was your relationship with your mother as a youth, and what is it like today?**

Growing up, my mom was really like my best friend. I remember she said she would bring me with her everywhere and we'd have the best time. As a kid, she helped me discover my eclectic musical taste when she would play albums by Tribe Called Quest, Sade & The Police. Now I definitely feel there's more distance in our relationship. She rarely opens up to me about anything that might really be going on in her life, and it's now come to a point where I pray she's doing fine, staying healthy and happy but no longer feel the need to pry for more details. We only speak on occasions and see each other on holidays and birthdays.

**Q. Is there anything you wish your dad did differently in rearing you?**

I wish that early on, when he saw my passion for music that he took my interest a bit more seriously and helped put the right resources around me to flourish. I'm not sure if he genuinely believed that my heart was in it and saw music as a way I could live out my dreams. My dad is very practical which, as a parent, I can totally understand. Sometimes we do need our parents to really champion us and be in our corner when it seems like the life we choose to live might not be the one they had in mind for us.

**Q. How has your dad helped shape/nurture your career?**

Like I mentioned his practical side—he definitely showed me that first and foremost, I have a duty to provide my child with the best possible upbringing, which helped me see the logic in finding a career path that more suits this way of thinking. As a project manager, I can still combine my love for social interaction and connecting with people in a way that benefits my company and clients I serve.

**Q. What mantras do you live by?**

One of the mantras I created as my vision for my music production company was "Elevate the Aura." That's what I try to live by. Our thoughts are the most powerful asset we have, and when we think on a higher level, I believe that we have the power to change our lives for the better just by changing our mindset.

**Q. How has Nia changed your life?**

Nia, 100%, saved my life. I couldn't imagine where I'd be without her. Around the time she was born, I was moving too fast... busy but not really productive in life. I felt like my party life persona was never going to catch up to me, and it did. I had a serious choice to make: either it was time to change the way I was living my life (partying all the time, drinking excessively, chasing women), and step up to be a father or I was going to wind up in jail or worse. I actually had to miss six months out of her life the February after she was born due to a DUI charge. This made me realize that there's someone other than myself counting on me to take the right path, and I feel I made the right decision.

**Q. What things are you planning to do with your own children that were important to you?**

Most important to me is to instill in my children to stand tall and dream big! I want her to fully immerse herself into whatever she is passionate about, and I will be there in her corner the whole way, helping to give her guidance.

# CHAPTER 15

# THICKER THAN WATER

*"The love of our family grows strong and deep*
*leaving memories to treasure and keep."*
***— Bill Davis***

Communication is the foundation of our family's survival. There were and still are times when we struggle to understand each other or be understood. In order to build a healthy home space where everyone felt safe emotionally and physically, communication was essential during those times when one person was upset. We had to find a way to act and disagree with each other constructively.

Of course, there was the teasing and bickering, but once it was clear that there would be no siblings beating up on each other, we had to find another way. Strong communication has become an intergenerational effort. I smile when I hear Sekou say to my granddaughter, "Nia, use your words," when she starts whining. I'm grateful that our communication has allowed us to build and maintain loving relationships—it definitely was not easy, lol.

AFRICA

## Staying Connected

**From:** bill <xxx>
**Sent:** Wednesday, January 3, 2018, 8:09 PM
**To:** xxx@gmail.com; xxx@gmail.com; xxx@yahoo.com; xxx@gmail.com; xxx@gmail.com
**Subject:** happy new year

Happy 2018 and Kwanzaa --love y'all hope everyone is healthy and enjoying the privilege of a new beginning. As we start the new year, we all hope for an improvement over the previous one. There are things that will make 2018 better:

Sekou will do better with a job back in NJ -- to which there has been some progress on this goal. I saw Debbie recently, and she is still planning to help despite her recent retirement. Glad the human resource rep is also interested in helping to make your relocation happen. In addition to the financial benefit, having more time with Nia will be tremendous. Nia is our fam fav we all hope that you will make the move to NJ soon; this will enable you to get Nia in some of the activities that help her development. And we are all inspired by your calm demeanor despite the weight you carry. Hopefully, there are some healthy ways to release the stress of 4 hours of commuting and financial challenges and the uncertainty of your relationship. During the holidays, we discussed the fact that you are only responsible for Nia, but you have also decided to support xxx. There is some concern about this decision supporting xxx. We all hope it will resolve itself in a healthy way. You deserve to be happy with someone who can also help contribute to your goals.

Toussaint I/we appreciated your clear and honest statements during Kwanzaa -- you and I have had conversations about your heart. We all hope you will be open to love again despite the recent challenges; a paradox you face is that as you become successful in your position, it will make you wonder if the lady is truly interested in you or your financial success. Glad you are not stressing as much about your supervisor and that your friends have helped you refocus and maintain your balance. Really happy you're consistent about going to the gym. It is a healthy way to cope and release stress. As you prepare to study for the exam and possibly start your own business, we will always support you and help as much as possible. I've had to make adjustments regarding this because I've limited ability to support you -- but hope you know I will in whatever way is best.

Imani congrats on your promotion I/we are very proud that you made this accomplishment in such a short time. We were and still hope you will be able to work in the NY/NJ area, but at this time, the universe intends for you to stay in Portland. The expectations for your success are very high. Please maintain your balance and don't stress too much. It will take time and some resources to fulfill the goals. I also hope you will continue your physical fitness activities, thanks again for inviting us to the marathon, it was an awesome experience. Your relationship situation is similar to Toussaint as your financial status improves finding someone just interested in you becomes somewhat more of a challenge. Despite these challenges, I think both of you will meet someone you love. Also glad you found some ‘ Black folks’ out there having some people who understand keeps us grounded is a blessing. I wish we could be with each other this week but unfortunately, we won’t until your next visit. I am going to visit you out there sometime this year.

Naeemah, aka Dream I/we believe 2018 will be better. It was amazing to see you overcome last years’ challenges and maintain a hopeful perspective. Our collective ability to overcome adversity has been and will always be a skill and strength we need. Hopefully, during the ‘sibling’ conversation, some ideas/strategies will be advanced that we can all support. Improving your infrastructure re a small SUV and finding a kitchen for large orders is high on the list. Also, increasing folks who can/will work with you. When we spoke recently you had some people to follow up with to accomplish some of these things if I can help let me know. Being creative about how you build Sweet Dreams will be a real asset. Also, staying healthy, not sure what your physical fitness activities are, but hopefully, you will develop a plan and stay with it. Maat is the philosophy of balance and justice. I/we hope you will strive to maintain your balance -- building your business is one aspect of life, but maintaining all of the others is important.

xxx, I/we all hope you are well and will reconnect. It has been too long since there has been any communication, but we all send positive energy to you -- love ya stay well.

I’m excited and nervous about retiring, but I’m ready for whatever the next phase of the journey will be. Writing the book and traveling will be a high priority. Each of us has and is currently building to accomplish our goals -- we are fortunate if and when there are folks who help us. I’m working and hoping the universe is going to help build the village I need to write -- as we've talked about the ideal situation is for someone to interview all of us and help glean the aspects of this journey that would help some folks especially young brothers. I'm humbled and honored to be able to take this next step. It's hard to believe that this year will be 41 years of working wow. Working with some of the folks has been a profound blessing --

Love y'all if you desire I can participate in your sibling conversation -- just call a brother lol --

Peace and Blessings

---

**From:** bill davis
**Sent:** Saturday, June 22, 2019 12:35 PM
**To:** xxx@gmail.com; xxx@gmail.com; xxx@gmail.com; xxx@yahoo.com; xxx@gmail.com
**Subject:** grateful

Hotep hope everyone is well, especially after Nia's graduation ceremony. Truly grateful for all of us to be there to celebrate and support Nia and Sekou. I'm grateful for how we love and support each other -- it is a great blessing.

Naeemah, I'm glad you are healthy and moving sweet dreams forward -- keep building, sometimes it will be difficult but stay at it.

Imani, your star is shining bright. The decision to stay at Nike and in Portland was definitely wise - safe travels.

Toussaint glad you are in love, it's been a long time, and we are happy to see you happy. Your next steps will happen when the universe intends for it to happen, be patient.

Sekou, glad you are honoring the fatherhood legacy -- we are all happy to be part of your and Nia's journey. They may be the strongest support group ever lol -- give thanks and praise. We are all praying for Pam and her dad; hopefully, his health will improve; and Pam will find a safe and affordable place.

I am also thankful for all of you and the blessings from the Creator. My first six months of 'retirement' have been a blessing and period of adjustment. I'm still on a work schedule ala waking up at the same time and doing work mainly at home. Next week the 'book' project will hopefully move forward -- my writing has been very slow. There are times when I wonder re the 5k to cover the cost, but given the many trips I've taken, I guess it will be a wise investment.

Reflecting on our conversation Sunday, I have a restless spirit, which has been reflected in these many journeys and relationships. There's a saying that when an artist is working on a project, they may not really know what the finished project will be and keep working to perfect it -- sometimes I feel this. Hopefully soon or when the Creator intends the people/place manifest -- it may be that my view may also have to evolve; I'm reminded of the saying 'the kingdom of heaven is within.'

Love y'all and grateful for our many blessings

---

**From:** Imani Davis <xxx@gmail.com>
**Sent:** Sunday, February 9, 2020, 7:54 PM
**To:** bill davis <xxx@hotmail.com>
**Cc:** Sekou Davis <xxx@yahoo.com>; tou <xxx@gmail.com>; dream <xxx@gmail.com>; xxx@gmail.com
**Subject:** Re: In the spirit of gratitude

Happy Sunday, y'all. So glad I got to FaceTime with the BROTHAS this morning. Glad y'all had a good time last night! Good wholesome fun. Also glad I got to catch up with Nae yesterday for an hour and a half! Just like old times! Looking forward to catching up with you later today, Baba.

Sekou, I love this email so much. I am going to read it once a week to remind myself of all of the love and support we have for each other and how far all of us have come. Now more than ever, we are all on our own individual journeys, but this note is a reminder that no matter what each of us is going through, we will always have each other's backs. I am so damn proud of you. To see the father that you've become and how much it reminds me of Baba is remarkable. Nia has been nothing short of a miracle in your life and for our whole family. It's crazy to see how fast she's growing up, but the way she has maintained her joy and wonder has been inspiring to watch. We know she's in the best hands with you, in spite of everything else, and of course, we will all always be here to support. We definitely need more FaceTime check-ins and calls, so let's hold each other accountable for that. Love you.

Baba, you have always been our rock. You were especially mine over the last few months as I battled a deep sadness I didn't know I was capable of experiencing. You helped me get through it by always checking on me, talking to me for hours, sending me uplifting songs and messages. I so appreciated your support throughout this period. We are all so lucky to have you as the leader of our clan, and I can't wait for the day I can buy you a house/vacation/whatever you want as the tiniest token of gratitude for everything you've ever done for all of us. We will never be able to pay you back, but we can certainly try. Soon!!! Love you.

Toussaint, my twin. I've always looked up to you so much (literally and figuratively, ha ha aaa) from following in your b-school/corporate footsteps to stealing your friends. 🙂 I'm so excited about your next step at a place that will value you and all of the skills and experiences that you bring to the table. I'm glad that you will get some time to chill before you start your next gig. Bring your ass to Portland so we can have some fun! 🎉 Seriously, thank you for showing me the blueprint, and being an inspiration, mentor and friend. Love you.

Naeemah, girl, I love you. I probably leaned on you the most during the last few months when I was so sad I didn't know what to do with myself. But you always provided some light for me, and I can't thank you enough for being there for me even as you were going through your own struggles. Your strength and resilience have served as an inspiration for me and showed me that I could get through ANYTHING. I am so happy that you have found a partner to go on life's journey with Chuck. I have to admit that for a while, it was hard to accept that I wasn't the first person you were turning to anymore, but I am getting better at accepting it (smile). I'm excited about the next step for Sweet Dreams. As you continue to iterate on your plan, know that I am here for you and will support your endeavors to the best of my ability -- always. Love you, my girl.

Man, this note took some time (and some tears!) to get through writing! I know you guys have been worried about me, but I want you to know that I have been really taking care of myself and am in a much better place now than I was even a month ago. I can't thank each of you individually or as a collective for supporting me during a pretty dark time. I've gotten through it because of the love and support from all of you. I love y'all so much, and I love us as a family.

Have a powerful week.
Hugs,
Imani

On Fri, Jan 31, 2020, at 8:11 AM bill davis <xxx@hotmail.com> wrote:
WOW, what a great way to start the day -- your love and message are very profound and inspires all of us to continue on our path. And if there's anything we can do to help just say it -- love y'all

---

**From:** Sekou Davis <xxx@yahoo.com>
**Sent:** Friday, January 31, 2020, 10:54 AM
**To:** baba <xxx@hotmail.com>; tou <xxx@gmail.com>; dream <xxx@gmail.com>; mani moo <xxx@gmail.com>; xxx@gmail.com
**Subject:** In the spirit of gratitude

Family,

These past few days have been hard to process. The last two nights, I've been awaken from my sleep with a lot on my heart. I've felt this before... I know where this unease stems from. But now, my ability to cope and work through these feelings are much better. And honestly, I owe that all to you. We have been through our own personal challenges, but each battle we face as a unit & rise above the circumstances. I cry, thanking God for each one of you and pray that the creator continues to bless us with health & happiness.

Baba, I love you. You are the truest leader by example and will always be our rock. I owe all of my abilities as a father to the lessons you've instilled in me. I plan to continue this journey with your wisdom to guide me. Man, it's not always easy... to stay patient when Nia isn't listening. When I come home to my house out of order & everyone is just chillin. I used to think, "why is Baba trippin?!" I GET IT! Lol, it all makes sense now... oh, and that Nia Songbook is on the way.

Toussaint, I love you. When I think about that "Mamba Mentality," I think of you. It was probably around '03 when Jay-Z "Moment of Clarity" dropped and you recited the lyrics to me:

Thank God for giving me this moment of clarity/ think moment of honesty... I'll never forget, I could see that something sparked in you. I think it was around that time where you told yourself you're prepared to outwork everyone in order to get to your dreams & goals. And through it all, your spirit & essence remains intact. You are the most selfless person I know, and I'm so grateful for you brother. Thank you.

Imani, I love you. It was this time last year that I was making plans to visit you in Portland. I remember riding thinking about how your positive spirit shines so bright here and how everyone marvels at your superpowers. I was "Imani's brother" and man that made me smile! That was a perfect weekend. I want you to know that even though we're 3,000 miles away, I am always here for you. I want to be more present for you, sis. More FaceTime calls & check-ins...Also, it's time we plan another trip your way with Nia this time. Also: "**remind yourself: Nobody built like you; you designed yourself!**"

Naeemah, I love you. I think back to our conversations about how important it is to follow our passions. You are a living testament to that, and I am so proud of your progression! Growing a business is one of the hardest but rewarding things ever. But you've made a decision. You can't stop, won't stop. And because of that decisiveness, the universe will make a path for you to follow to your destiny. It's because of you that I'm ready to get back into producing again, this time with the sole purpose of simply doing what I love. Thank you.

Nia, I love you. Thank you for saving my life. Thank you for choosing me. God only knows what my life would be like now without you.

You've taught me to be more open, honest and loving. You are a special child. Everyone sees it. Please maintain that kind & thoughtful spirit for as long as you can. Things in this world will become more difficult as time goes on, but know that I will always have your back. Know that Baba, Uncle Tou, Auntie Moo & Nae will always be there. We are only starting out on this journey, and I hope I'm doing a good job so far. I will continue to work on being more patient, and I pray that I can help you fulfill whatever dreams you may have. Whether it's a dancer, an engineer, a comedian baby, you will be the best ever! You can do ANYTHING!!!

I am so grateful. Please, God, continue to protect our family. Continue to bring each one of us closer to our purpose. Let the ancestors guide us with their wisdom & let's let love lead the way.

Amen. Ashe.

Sent from my iPhone

# CHAPTER 16

# MY REDEMPTION SONG

*"But my hand was made strong*
*By the hand of the almighty*
*We forward in this generation*
*Triumphantly*
*Won't you help to sing*
*These songs of freedom?*
*'Cause all I ever have*
*Redemption songs*
*Redemption songs*
*Emancipate yourselves from mental slavery*
*None but ourselves can free our minds..."*
***— Bob Marley***

As parents, we all make sacrifices. I was blessed to have a career in education and still be present in my children's daily lives. Sacrifice is a significant part of parenting. It's based on a historical precedent each generation creates a way to build an environment for their children to grow and prosper. My journey taught me to love in ways that enriched my life. Helping my crew through the various challenges, and seeing the outcome is more than fulfilling.

Helping children and young adults resolve issues of peer pressure is a significant emotional journey. Society perpetuates the idea of 'worth' by material wealth and or items that reflect it. Our collective self-esteem as a society and as people of African ancestry at times needs to be strengthened. One of my favorite MLK speeches is about the overemphasis on materialism. The country could never fulfill its ideal of liberty and justice as long as the focus on materialism was so great.

One of the great challenges of my parent journey is seeing behavior in your children and not knowing what steps to take to change and improve it. If we're lucky, time and persistence will lead to improving it. Our culture teaches people to focus on individual achievement and satisfaction; parenting requires thinking and working for a collective solution.

Whatever sacrifices I made were small, relative to knowing that I was honoring the parental tradition, whether economic, financial, professional, or personal. Since I was being blamed for the failure of my marriage and judged by what happened with my Crew, then doing what was needed to raise them was my primary concern.

*"When we live our lives in love, we find a way to make the important things in life work."*
**— Bill Davis**

As I have mentioned, if it were not for the "village," it's highly unlikely that my Crew and I would have made it this far. More importantly, if Marilyn had not agreed with the decision to allow me to raise them in a healthy environment, then their future may not have turned out as positive. I owe Marilyn a huge amount of gratitude for her love for our children and her courage to make a tough decision.

*Dear Marilyn,*

*Thank you so much for your support over these many years. I sincerely appreciate your quiet prayers and encouragement – it fits your personality.*

*Your support and prayers have been very helpful to the Crew and especially me. There is a certain peace in knowing that someone is praying for you and wishing you well. One of the most helpful things to the Crew was that they were not receiving conflicting messages. Your message to them was to excel and manifest their multiple talents. Especially for Imani and Naeemah in their aspiration and imagination about following your tradition of being in the fashion industry. This was extremely helpful as young ladies often struggle with appreciating their beauty.*

*The blessing of your Mom is also something that we are profoundly grateful for. Loretta has been one of our guardian angels. I'm sure you remember that right after your Mom passed, Naeemah's heart condition was diagnosed. We were fortunate to have healthcare coverage and competent doctors to save Dream's life.*

*I'm also especially grateful for your trust. The Crew is our collective contribution to eternity. Thank you for trusting me to raise them. Your sacrifice was a significant contribution to their success.*

*Thank you so much – Asante Sana.*

*Peace and Blessings*

# Epilogue

Saturday, May 30, 2020, New Jersey has 159,608k coronavirus cases and 11,634k deaths. It's been exactly four weeks since our family has been traumatized by COVID-19. My nephew fought back the tears as he witnessed the John F. Kennedy medical staff in Edison, put his mom on a ventilator. All of us are frightened, as the uncertainty about what comes next is agonizing. Like many other states, New Jersey has placed restrictions on visiting family and loved ones in the hospital and nursing homes. The policy is intended to "flatten the curve" of the virus. It is understandable from the public health perspective, but it creates significant anxiety and tension for family members.

Our family is one of the thousands of African American families infected by the virus. The disproportionate impact has had a devastating effect on families and communities' physical, emotional, and financial circumstances that will have negative generational consequences. Despite the coronavirus's health risks, I went to protest the virus of racism and police brutality with thousands of others. In addition to restrictions regarding hospitals and nursing homes, New Jersey, among other states, has issued "shelter in place or stay at home" directives. But witnessing the brutal murder of George Floyd, I was inspired by many of our ancestors; Malcolm, Martin, Mandela, Harriet, Fannie Lou, Frederick, among others. Being at the protest was cathartic and a step toward healing. Mayor Ras Baraka and Larry Hamm were two of the many speakers who encouraged us to fight injustice. Seeing so many people defy the restrictions was encouraging because the spirit of resistance was definitely alive. In a historical context there are protests in over 100 cities and abroad which is the first time since the assassination of Dr. King. This current protest brought back memories of the first protest/riot in Plainfield, ironically over the same issue of police brutality.

As I complete this book, these current crises are a discerning reminder of the racism and police brutality virus that has infected the country for hundreds of years. It is a profound reminder of the challenge of parenting African American children in this climate. The anxiety of your children being a victim of police or racist violence is ever-present. My hope for all African Americans and other parents of color is to honor the tradition of overcoming these challenges and to the best of their ability create a healthy environment to raise their children.

I hope that more Black fathers tell their stories to help change the narrative of the absent Black father's myth. The negative stereotypes of Black fathers' lack of involvement in their children's lives due to incarceration, drugs, or laziness are false. Yet, these statements and images are regularly portrayed by the mass media. Black fathers are present, and studies show that they are more involved in daily care, such as bathing, feeding, dressing, homework, and playtime.[5] We love our children, just like any other race or ethnicity. Where do we go from here? Forward. Black Fathers let's stand up together!

*Aluta Continua – the struggle continues.*

*"But my hand was made strong*
*By the hand of the almighty*
*We forward in this generation*
*Triumphantly..."*

**— Bob Marley**

# ABOUT THE AUTHOR

William Davis Jr., more popularly known as Bill Davis and affectionately called "Brother Black," is a Newark native who was raised and educated in Plainfield. A significant event that impacted his journey was witnessing the rebellion, aka riots in Plainfield in 1967. This protest was one of the factors that would shape his trajectory relative to expanding his knowledge and increased his involvement in the quest for freedom and justice. His mother, Mrs. Charlotte Davis, an advocate for African American culture and justice, was instrumental in his cultural development.

Bill attended Rutgers as an EOF student and majored in Africana Studies. As an undergraduate, Bill served as the President of the Students for Afro American Society, was a member of B.U.S.T. - Blacks United to Save Themselves, and wrote for the Black Voice, among other activities. The Rutgers climate was hostile for African American students, and the attrition rate was very high. There were many protests which he participated in; one of the more memorable was the 'basketball game' protest whereby the game was stopped to demand improvement in conditions for African American students. One of the notable activities was the 'Tribute to the Black Man of America' ceremony, which was an effort to highlight the contributions of students and staff. Bill, among others, coordinated the event.

After graduation, Bill was hired as an admissions counselor at Rutgers Camden with a focus on recruiting African American, Latino, and EOF students. He was appointed with the help of two mentors; Don

Phifer and Willie Hamm. During his undergraduate year, he had the good fortune to work in admissions as a student recruiter.

Following his time in Camden, Bill was transferred to the New Brunswick campus and worked in EOF central office under the direction of Richard Nurse. During this time, there were again numerous protests on campus to end apartheid in South Africa. Honoring the great tradition of our ancestors, he actively participated in these protests.

Upon a transfer to the Newark campus, Bill served as an EOF counselor and as the advisor to BOS - the Black Organization of Students. As the protest against apartheid continued, Bill, along with several others, started a male group to improve graduation rates. After joining a few community organizations, he began to work with others for justice and became actively involved in the 1984 Jackson campaign. At the request of Lennox Hinds, Bill participated in the planning and convening of the first national anti-apartheid conference held in the country at Riverside church.

Bill served as the founding Assistant Director of the Office for African American Student Services at New York University prior to his return to New Jersey, where he served as Director of the New Brunswick campus for Middlesex County College. During his tenure on the New Brunswick campus, he worked on the pre-college consortium project, which provided educational experiences for 7th-12th grade Newark students. He created a pre-college program in Piscataway based on this model, Epic Vision Academy. Piscataway is a diverse community, but African American students were underachieving, and Epic provided students needed support to enhance their academic performance.

Bill also served as a training and consultant specialist at the Boggs Center on Developmental Disabilities at Rutgers Robert Wood Johnson

Medical School. As a single parent for the past 23 years, he is the proud father of five adult children, all of whom are also Rutgers alumni. He is also a proud grandparent of Nia, who has brought his family immense joy. His parenting philosophy was greatly shaped by his father, William Sr., whose role in Bill's life and their family was profound as they were all touched by William Sr. 's care and concern. Bill was fortunate to have parents who loved him and his siblings and whose lessons were instrumental in all of our lives.

In January 2019, Bill semi-retired after 41 years of working in the 'vineyard'; he was ready to explore a few other options—first, to write about the amazing journey and blessings that have manifested in his life. Secondly, to work with young men around various issues, including parenting and navigating the journey of being an African American man in America. Bill continuously attempts to live his life by the philosophy of lifting as we climb. In tribute to those who were instrumental in his development, his lifelong goal is to pay it forward and honor our great ancestor's traditions.

Last but not least, he is profoundly grateful to his children, aka "the Crew" who have been the wind beneath his wings. He is also grateful to his former wife for her decision to allow him to raise the Crew, although difficult, her choice benefitted them. To the 'folks' in the village, Asante Sana, your support and assistance will always be immensely appreciated.

# FURTHER ACKNOWLEDGMENTS

## TRIP TO THE MOTHERLAND

*"A man with no knowledge of himself is like a tree without roots."*

— **Dick Gregory**

There are many additional people to salute and express my profound gratitude and appreciation. The people of South Africa who sacrificed so much in their heroic fight for freedom; their efforts certainly inspired many around the world then and now. A special note of thanks to Comrade Raks and his family for their generous hospitality, sharing their wisdom, and allowing me to meet stalwarts of the anti-apartheid struggle. The children and students who are so energetic and hopeful despite the challenges they face relative to facilities and obstacles, they honor our long tradition of being resilient and lifting as we climb. The brothers in GLP for their efforts to contribute to the children and communities, Asante Sana I salute you and hope we will continue to collaborate on future initiatives. To my family and extended family and many 'folks' who contributed to my journey, they donated books, money and sent much positive energy and prayers for a safe and healthy trip, thanks so much I am sincerely grateful. To my children, I am proud of you. I love you, and I hope you realize that this trip was possible because all of you are who you are.

*Aluta Continua In Thando (love - Zulu) and peace*

# RESOURCES

For books, videos, and other materials about African American history visit: www.babaslegacy.com. Below is my syllabus for teaching Africana Studies which also contains great reading material.

**INTRODUCTION TO AFRICANA STUDIES**
SPRING 2018
01:014:103:02 * MW 5-6:20 SERC 203
INSTRUCTOR: WILLIAM DAVIS

**Course Description:**
This course places the lives and stories of people of African descent at the center of the narrative and as the basis of historical analysis. The objective of this course is to give students a general overview of the history of Africa and its (Diaspora) peoples using a variety of intellectual lenses. We will look at the economic, political, and social developments that shaped the Black Diaspora and analyze the culture and institutional arrangements shared by people of African descent in different parts of the world. The course is designed so that each student can gain an appreciation of continuities and changes that have taken place from the seventeenth millennium BCE up to the present.

The course is organized thematically. This is a course about historical processes and how and why an event occurs and if specific events have any important connections to any series of other episodes or circumstances Throughout Semester extra credit assignments can be arranged. Students are expected to complete reading assignments before the beginning of each class to enhance class participation.

Participation in class discussions is highly encouraged and rewarded. Students are expected to do all assignments within the rules of academic integrity.

**Required Texts:**

Clay Carson, Gary Nash, Emma Lapsansky-Wemer, eds. (2004) African American Lives, The Struggle for Freedom, Single Volume Edition. Longman: New York
(ISBN: 0-3210-2586-5)
Various Handouts: To Be Provided via Rutgers Libraries On-Line Reserve

**Course Goals:**

To develop an understanding and knowledge of Africana Studies as an evolving multidisciplinary field.

To understand the nature of classical African civilizations and their relationship to the rest of the world in the past and the present; To develop knowledge and understanding of the history and processes that creates the African Diaspora including the motivation and processes that lead to the enslavement of African Peoples as well as the struggle for emancipation and against racism in the Americas; To develop an understanding of the history of and appreciation for Black aesthetics and the arts as well as developing knowledge and understanding of the ideas and philosophies of outstanding thinkers, writers, leaders, and artists of African ancestry; To understand the role of African cultural and spiritual retentions in the Americas and the African presence in (North and South) American cultures.

To understand the global struggle of African peoples for freedom including the struggle against colonialism and apartheid.

## THE BLACK FAMILY

**Course Description:**

This course places the lives and stories of people of African descent at the center of the narrative and as the basis of historical analysis of issues regarding the black family. The objective of this course is to give students a general historical overview of the institutional factors that affect the structure, evolution and function of the African American family in the US. Students will explore historical issues relating to the past and present life circumstances of African American families. Some exploration of Africa and the Diaspora will enhance students' understanding; some topics that will be addressed include: nuclear versus extended family; two parent and female headed households; in addition to urban versus suburban/rural families.

Throughout the semester extra credit assignments can be arranged. Students are expected to complete reading assignments before the beginning of each class to enhance class participation.

Participation in class discussions is highly encouraged and rewarded. Students are expected to do all assignments within the rules of academic integrity review RU policy.

**Required Texts**:

Hattery, A. & Smith (2007). African American Families Thousand Oaks, Ca; Sage Publications

Jewell, K. Sue (2003) Survival of the African American Family Praeger Publishers, CT: Greenwood Publishing Group

Is Marriage for White People (2011) Dutton Publishers, NY

Various Handouts: To Be Provided via Rutgers Libraries On-Line Reserve

**Course Goals**:

To develop an understanding and knowledge of Africana Studies as an evolving multidisciplinary field of study. To develop knowledge and understanding of the history and processes that creates the African American Family and to develop strategies that will enhance the understanding and functioning of the family; including personal choices, financial literacy and policy examination.

**FOR BOOKINGS AND MORE INFORMATION VISIT:**

**www.babaslegacy.com**

AFRICA

# Endnotes

1. https://www.nj.com/politics/2016/06/nj_has_12_times_more_black_prisoners_than_white_on.html

2. https://luskin.ucla.edu/how-america-became-the-worlds-largest-jailer

3. https://www.sentencingproject.org/publications/color-of-justice-racial-and-ethnic-disparity-in-state-prisons/

4. https://www.latimes.com/politics/la-na-pol-2020-school-segregation-busing-harris-biden-20190708-story.html

5. https://www.youtube.com/watch?v=9-nYUUhigTU

AFRICA

Made in the USA
Middletown, DE
15 February 2023

24507895R00137